FAMILY PORTRA

T0154328

BOOKS BY ROBERT ALEXANDER

What the Raven Said: Poems (2006)

Five Forks: Waterloo of the Confederacy—A Civil War Narrative (2003)

White Pine Sucker River: Poems 1970–1990 (1993)

OTHER ANTHOLOGIES

The House of Your Dream: An International Collection of Prose Poetry
edited by Robert Alexander and Dennis Maloney *(2008)*

The Talking of Hands: Unpublished Writing by New Rivers Press Authors
edited by Robert Alexander, Mark Vinz,
and C. W. Truesdale *(1998)*

The Party Train: A Collection of North American Prose Poetry
edited by Robert Alexander, Mark Vinz,
and C. W. Truesdale *(1996)*

FAMILY PORTRAIT

American Prose Poetry
1900–1950

Edited by Robert Alexander

With an introduction by Margueritte S. Murphy

WHITE PINE PRESS / BUFFALO, NEW YORK

Cover: Charles Sheeler, American, 1883–1965. *L C Smith Typewriter.* Negative
date: 1920s. Photograph, gelatin silver print. Sheet: 28.5 x 40.2 cm (11 1/4
x 15 13/16 in.). Mount: 36.4 x 45.7 cm (14 5/16 x 18 in.) Copyright © The
Lane Collection. Courtesy, Museum of Fine Arts, Boston.

First Edition.

Printed and bound in the United States of America.

ISBN 978-1-893996-35-1

Printed and bound in the United States of America

Library of Congress Control Number: 2012931166

THE MARIE ALEXANDER POETRY SERIES, VOLUME 16

Published by
White Pine Press
P.O. Box 236
Buffalo, NY 14201
www.whitepine.org

The poem in prose is the form of the future.
—Charles Henri Ford

Contents

LIST OF AUTHORS BY BIRTH DATE

Amy Lowell, 1874–1925
Gertrude Stein, 1874–1946
Sherwood Anderson, 1876–1941
Robert Alden Sanborn, 1877–1966
William Carlos Williams, 1883–1963
Jane Heap, 1883–1964
John Gould Fletcher, 1886–1950
H. D., 1886–1961
Margaret C. Anderson, 1886–1973
Fenton Johnson, 1888–1958
T. S. Eliot, 1888–1965
Harriet Dean, 1892–1964
E. E. Cummings, 1894–1962
Jean Toomer, 1894–1967
Robert McAlmon, 1896–1956
William Faulkner, 1897–1962
Thornton Wilder, 1897–1975.
Harry Crosby, 1898–1929
Ernest Hemingway, 1899–1961
Emily Holmes Coleman, 1899–1974
Laura Riding, 1901–1991
Kay Boyle, 1902–1992
Charles Henri Ford, 1908–2002
Edouard Roditi, 1910–1992
Paul Bowles, 1910–1999
Kenneth Patchen, 1911–1972
Mary Fabilli, 1914–2011
Virginia Admiral, 1915–2000
Robert Duncan, 1919–1988
Holly Beye, 1922–2011

EDITOR'S NOTE

It's a common notion these days that the prose poem is a johnny-come-lately to the dance of American poetry. A fairly haphazard search yielded, for example, the following sentence on a website maintained by the Academy of American Poets:

> It was not until the post–War period, over a hundred years after its French debut, that the prose poem was actively taken up by American poets; in the American tradition of innovation, it's a latecomer, with its first great boom occurring in the seventies.[1]

I'd agree that the seventies were the first truly boom years for the prose poem, but American poets had written a great variety of prose poetry before that. Much of this work originally appeared in so-called little magazines and other ephemeral small-press publications, and to this day much of it has never been reprinted. Even prose poems by such well-known authors as H. D. and William Carlos Williams have for some reason gone missing from their collected works.

What this anthology consists of, broadly speaking, is short pieces of prose by American writers from the first half of the twentieth century. The earliest work here is from Gertrude Stein's *Tender Buttons,* published in 1914—the year that signaled so brutally the end of one era and the beginning of another—and the most recent work dates from the early fifties, during the era of nuclear fear which helped precipitate a different sea-change in American literature. Because I've limited this selection to poets born before 1925, it excludes the work of those like Robert Bly and Allen Ginsberg, who in any case are part of another cultural generation. Overall, I've aimed at a selection of work based not on its historical interest alone, but rather on the strength of its literary quality— a sampling of the best prose poems of the flowering of American Modernism.

The abundance of prose poems from the first decades of the century ranges from Stein's language experiments to more narrative works such as Ernest Hemingway's "In Our Time." There's a good dose of surrealism from writers such as Charles Henri Ford and Edouard Roditi; there are slice-of-life sketches from Robert Alden Sanborn and Kay Boyle, who also gives us emotionally charged image-sequences. Some work, such as that by H. D. and John Gould Fletcher, is written with a more traditionally poetic diction, while other writers such as Emily Holmes Coleman and Laura Riding explore the boundaries between fiction and poetry.

In contrast to the fertile years which produced this wealth of achievement, the two decades from 1930 to 1950 provide a relative scarcity of American prose poems. John Gould Fletcher, in speaking of the different sort of emphasis occasioned by the Crash of 1929, said that while beforehand little magazines were "prevailingly aesthetic, the later crop has been in many cases imbued with proletarian protest, with an atmosphere of Marxism."[2] This change did not bode well for experimental forms such as the prose poem, though the advent of James Laughlin's New Directions in 1936 provide an outlet for much new writing. Indeed, one has only to look at Kenneth Patchen's writing (published in part by New

Directions) to see that the tradition of American experimental prose doesn't disappear in the thirties and forties. Also in the forties, a coterie of writers—including Robert Duncan, Virginia Admiral, and Mary Fabilli—publish in the *Experimental Review*, but in general the Depression and subsequent World War created pressures that didn't leave a lot of room for what was still a marginal form in America. In the fifties, another era of experimentation begins, but that's beyond the scope of this anthology—with the exception of Holly Beye, who early in the decade focused on prose poems, and others like Patchen who had already worked in the form. William Carlos Williams is exceptional in being represented among both the earliest and the latest work in this anthology, as his efforts in short prose extend throughout his long career.

Many of the writers in this collection are well-known in the annals of Modernism, but others are less familiar. What bears emphasizing is that in putting together this anthology, I had a surfeit of authors and poems to choose from. For every piece included here, there are many others I had no space for, and no doubt many others I never found. In my opinion, nearly a century now after the publication of *Tender Buttons*, the prose poem deserves to be recognized for its small though significant place in our national canon.

1. Volkman 2003.
2. Hoffman et. al. 1946, 154–155.

Introduction: The Prose Poem as a Modernist Genre

Margueritte S. Murphy

I began to wonder at at about this time just what
one saw when one looked at anything really
looked at anything. Did one see sound, and what
was the relation between color and sound, did it
make itself by description by a word that meant it
or did it make itself by a word in itself. . . .

—Gertrude Stein on the composition of
Tender Buttons ("Portraits and Repetition,"
Lectures in America)

I begin with this quotation from Gertrude Stein not only
because she produced some of the most startling and elusive prose
poems of the twentieth century in her collection, *Tender Buttons,* but
because the impulse she describes behind their writing leads us to
the heart of Modernist experimentation and to the value of the
prose poem to that generation of writers. It is a commonplace of
the history of Modernism that one of its preoccupations is the
question of representation, and Gertrude Stein famously took up
that question with Picasso as she sat for her portrait. She poses this
question of looking—at objects, at faces, at phenomena—as one
of interrogating the frameworks of observation as observation has
been conventionally practiced, and of recording these new observa-
tions differently, in this instance, of somehow discovering and con-

veying the sound of the thing embedded in the description. Such reframing was undoubtedly inspired by experiments in representation in other art forms—the difference in "looking" of Picasso's and Braque's Cubist paintings, for instance—but it is also impelled by modernity itself, that is, perceptions of a world and ways of life transformed, of places, spaces and experiences of time affected by new phenomena and technologies. For Stein, such wondering involves questioning and putting in question how language represents: and in this short passage, this wondering takes up the synesthetic dimension of experience and art, as she ponders how color represents; and the relationship between color and sound—in other words, the conversion of new ways of looking into a new language. She questions and then innovates and invents; the "product" employs a novel, transformational use of language. Modernity influences not only what one represents, but how representation can take place. There is also a consequence for the subject: reframings of "looking" unsettle the position and role of the observer; looking itself is an activity, a dynamic art.

While not every Modernist had the good fortune to sit for Picasso, such questions of representation were pervasive and pervade the collection of prose poems in this anthology, but in a wide variety of ways and degrees of intensity.[1] I would argue that the prose poem provided a particular, even unique, vehicle for the exploration of such central Modernist questions and themes. This is not to suggest that the prose poem was by any means the chief literary form for such exploration; clearly experimentation in the novel and free verse poetry produced the exemplary, indeed the canonical Modernist texts. Simply the prose poem, although hardly embraced by the most prominent Modernists,[2] in its typical brevity, offers a focus and intensity unfettered by other purposes—such as contribution to plot or situation in a novel, or the construction of cadence or the structure of line in verse poetry.[3] The choice of perspective, the angle chosen, for instance, shapes a prose poem dramatically; upsetting the representational applecart can be the central thrust of the text.

Stein's comment also reminds us of the close association that the prose poem has had since its origins with representation of the phenomenal world. This association is due in part to the prose poem's affiliation with painting and illustration; Baudelaire's own acknowledged forerunner, Aloysius Bertrand, subtitled his volume, *Gaspard de la nuit*, "Fantasies in the style of Rembrandt and Callot." The title of Arthur Rimbaud's *Illuminations* refers to "painted plates" according to Verlaine,[4] and playing off the conventions of description has been central to the prose poem since these nineteenth-century roots. With Modernism's fascination with exploring and capturing the moment—associated most prominently with Henri Bergson's philosophy and Marcel Proust's and Virginia Woolf's fiction—the prose poem proves to be an especially apt form for such "captures," a recording of object and affect.

This anthology holds many such examples, for instance, Amy Lowell's "Bath":

The day is fresh-washed and fair, and there is a smell
of tulips and narcissus in the air.
The sunshine pours in at the bathroom window and
bores through the water in the bathtub in lathes and

planes of greenish-white. It cleaves the water into flaws like a jewel, and cracks it to bright light.

Little spots of sunshine lie on the surface of the water and dance, dance, and their reflections wobble deliciously over the ceiling; a stir of my finger sets them whirring, reeling. I move a foot, and the planes of light in the water jar. I lie back and laugh, and let the green-white water, the sun-flawed beryl water, flow over me. The day is almost too bright to bear, the green water covers me from the too bright day. I will lie here awhile and play with the water and the sun spots.

The sky is blue and high. A crow flaps by the window, and there is a whiff of tulips and narcissus in the air.

The pose is one of careful observation yet playful enjoyment, a recording of the effect of sunlight on bathwater and the heightened sensations of the bather. The tropes of water as jewel and sunlight as boring tool portray liquid as a diamantine solid to be broken open, creating an impression of brilliance and the sunray's power; "flaws" in this "jewel" and "crack[ed]" "bright light" emphasize the sunlight's gorgeous shattering. The "poetry" as it were lies in such tropes and images and the rendition of the bather's sensations—the flowers' fragrance and movement of the water. While Lowell felt that rhyme ("fair"/"air"; "pours"/"bores"; "white"/"light" for instance) was essential to the prose's status as "polyphonic prose,"[5] it is rather the rendering of this experience in the bath, of light hitting the water, the verbal

Bonnard, as it were, that ties the piece to the Modernist exploration of how sensation affects consciousness and the Modernist celebration of the panoply of sensation during a brief period of time.

Beyond such close attention to the minutiae of sensation, other dominant themes in this collection reflect the preoccupations of the Modernists and their reactions to the world they lived in. One of these is the city: a rapidly changing environment during their lifetimes, one inspiring both fascination and dismay. The affiliation of the prose poem with the city is deeply rooted: the dual title of Charles Baudelaire's *Le Spleen de Paris (Petits poèmes en prose)*, the first widely recognized collection of prose poems, links the form and the city, and Baudelaire, in his dedication of the volume to Arsène Houssaye, acknowledges a forerunner in Aloysius Bertrand's *Gaspard de la nuit* with prose poems set in Dutch cities and Paris, albeit of the past. The prose poem affords a particular lens on the city: typically it is not the broad perspective, the diorama, or bird's-eye view that predominates, but detailed meditations on its corners and passages, narratives of fleeting and random experience on its sidewalks and streets, descriptions of activities peculiar to urban life (for instance, the deep flânerie celebrated in Baudelaire's "The Crowds"). In other words, this short poetic form provides a sharp focus and condensed scope conducive to rendering particular moments, scenes and experiences. The movement towards meaning or towards the general "truth" is in the telling detail and the narrator's reflections in the moment, or in retrospect about the moment, rather than the grand vista. The "spleen" of Baudelaire's Paris is portrayed through briefly encountered scenes and characters—the old clown in his stall ignored by the crowd ("The Old Clown"); the poor yet still lovely widow listening to the park concert at the periphery, outside the paid seating ("The Widows"); the eyes of the poor family looking into the new café that the speaker's unfeeling bourgeois lover complains of ("The Eyes of the Poor"). Urban experience is multiple, random, and fragmented; the prose poem emerges as a form suited to the depiction of singular, discrete moments in all their immediacy.

This potential and legacy are clear in the prose poems in this collection; by the early twentieth century, modernization had accelerated, and prose poems record its sounds as well as its sights. These prose poems in their "framings" portray a world that surprises with stark urban textures and deafening noise, and with the jolts of novel technologies. Amy Lowell's "Midday and Afternoon," for instance, captures the rhythms of sound and light in the daytime streets:

> Swirl of crowded streets. Shock and recoil of traffic. The stock-still brick façade of an old church, against which the waves of people lurch and withdraw. Flare of sunshine down side-streets. Eddies of light in the windows of chemists' shops, with their blue, gold, purple jars, darting colours far into the crowd. Loud bangs and tremors, murmurings out of high windows, whirring of machine belts, blurring of horses and motors. A quick spin and shudder of brakes on an electric car, and the jar of a church-bell knocking against the metal blue of the sky. I am a piece of the town, a bit of blown dust,

thrust along with the crowd. Proud to feel the pavement under me, reeling with feet. Feet tripping, skipping, lagging, dragging, plodding doggedly, or springing up and advancing on firm elastic insteps. A boy is selling papers, I smell them clean and new from the press. They are fresh like the air and pungent as tulips and narcissus.

The blue sky pales to lemon, and great tongues of gold blind the shop-windows, putting out their contents in a flood of flame.

Lowell's nouns—"swirl," "shock and recoil," "waves," "eddies"— suggest patterns of activity with the remnant of an older city, the old church, as the still point against which they play. The sounds are a mixture, generated by machines, animals, people, and church bells. But modernity predominates for even the sky is cast as a "metal blue." The narrator exults in her fusion with the city and the crowd, losing her own will to direct her steps. It is also the record of transition between two phases of the day, and so as "blue sky pales to lemon," its light extinguishes the commercial display, the play of colors previously "darting . . . far into the crowd." Lowell has understood the lesson of Impressionism that light creates the scene and is as "real" as the more palpable objects. Ending with the annihilation of the scene by rays of sunlight is a Rimbaldian note, reminiscent of the ending of "The Bridges" (said to be a London-inspired prose poem): "A white ray, falling from the top of the sky, wipes out this bit of theatricality" (73). For all that the scene constitutes a new reality that millions experience, observed closely, it is fleeting, and the observation itself is as untrustworthy as it is creative.

Other prose poems focus predominantly on the sounds of the city, for instance, William Carlos Williams' "theessentialroar." In it a page-long sentence describes, simulates, and celebrates urban noise, connecting in a single stream its many "roars"—trains, films, traffic, the press, the ballpark. The "roar" fuses sentences; nothing is discrete: "It is the roar first brilliantly overdone THEN the plug in the pipe that carries them home with a ROAR and a cigarette and a belly full of sweet sugar and the roar of the film or to sit at the busy hour in the polished window of Union Club at the northeast corner of fifty-first street. . . ."

In the hands of e. e. cummings, such fusion puts an even greater strain on syntax in his prose poems that depict the sounds and sights of New York, as in this passage from "i was sitting in mcsorley's": "the Bar.tinking luscious jigs dint of ripe silver with warmlyish wetflat splurging smells waltz the glush of squirting taps plus slush of foam knocked off and a faint piddle-of-drops she say I ploc spittle what the lands thaz me kid in no sir hopping sawdust you kiddo he's a palping wreaths of badly Yep cigars who jim him why gluey grins topple together eyes pout gestures stickily point made glints squinting who's a wink bum-nothing and money fuzzily mouths take big wobbly foot-steps every goggle cent of it get out ears dribbles soft right old feller belch the chap hic summore eh chuckles skulch. . . ."[6] The description of the bar gives way to speech; the stream of words creates the sense of chaos in the bar and reflects a growing drunkenness which is also a drunkenness on language, on phonic play, amidst noise. Yet the evocation of this disorderly interior is set off and tempered by the contrasting note of the opening and ending of the prose poem, a scene of serenity based in the order of nature, even in New York, although at the end, cummings uses punctuation to disrupt even this lyricism: "outside(it was New York and beautifully, snowing. . . .")

In Robert Alden Sanborn's "Alleys," the focus is the quieter animation of night in the city. In contrast with the doglike diurnal street, "The street leaps upon me, breast-high, rampant, its greedy eyes lick at my face, I feel its heavy paws upon my body," the speaker seeks out the feline nocturnal alley. The alley is a "small shadowy hush"; "I can pick the alley up in my hands, it is limp and drowsy and unsuspecting. I can lay it down in a cushioned nook of memory, and still it lies." The city itself provides fellowship, not its inhabitants. One thinks of Atget's contemporaneous photographs of Paris, capturing the beauty of its empty streets, doorways, and facades.

With the prose poem and its challenge to the music of verse, there also arises the question of how or whether this is song. In Sherwood Anderson's "Song of the Soul of Chicago," the speaker proclaims that prose suits the medium of talk, not song, and that that fits the life of the urban underclass: "I'll talk forever—I'm damned if I'll sing. Don't you see that mine is not a singing people? We're just a lot of muddy things caught up by the stream. You can't fool us. Don't we know ourselves?" But here, too, is the promise of song: "By God we'll love each other or die trying. We'll get to understanding too. In some grim way our own song shall work through." The prose poem affords transcription of the full music of speech. ("We want to give this democracy thing they talk so big about a whirl.") Charles Henri Ford's "Suite" (published when he was in college in the magazine he founded, *Blues: A Magazine of New*

Rhythms)[7] suggests music not only through its title and its reference to Ethel Waters on the Victrola at the end, but also through, again, a rush of fused sentences into which fragments of others' language are spliced. This rushed music is identified as urban: "chicago is not a town to sneer at neither to grow sentimental over: you can stand under the el at five or fivethirty or six and talk as loud as you want to and nobody will hear you: at night walking on michigan avenue nobody will see you for the automobiles rush by too fast…" The city creates rhythms: human speech and the noise that drowns out human speech in spurts, resulting in a cacophony of the sounds of urban machinery and talk. The city bestows a glorious inaudibility and invisibility on the individual, while making itself incomprehensible.

If some of the prose poems referenced so far could be loosely characterized as descriptive, others in this anthology represent another major strain, that of the narrative prose poem, playing off the ancient tradition of moral tale. This form, in which ideally nothing is extraneous or wasted, mimics and discredits its modern counterparts, for instance, the social columns of the daily newspaper, the short gossipy item. The prose poem in contrast has weight; human actions have consequences without the explicit "moral" of traditional storytelling. Moreover, their implicit "morals" apply to a changed and changing world, whose reading is complicated by questions of how one knows as well as how one judges. For instance, in William Carlos Williams' *Kora in Hell: Improvisations,* the text alternates between plain type and italics, creating a counterpoint between the rendition of immediate experience and the reflection on that experience. These shifts in perspective produce texts that offer an especially clear illustration of how the prose poem can tell stories and the story of searching for their meaning:

What can it mean to you that a child wears pretty clothes and speaks three languages or that its mother goes to the best shops? It means: July has good need of his blazing sun. But if you pick one berry from the ash tree I'd not know it again for the same no matter how the rain washed. Make my bed of witchhazel twigs, said the old man, since they bloom on the brink of winter.

———————

There is neither beginning nor end to the imagination but it delights in its own seasons reversing the usual order at will. Of the air of the coldest room it will seem to build the hottest passions. Mozart would dance with his wife, whistling his own tune to keep the cold away and Villon ceased to write upon his Petit Testament only when the ink was frozen. But men in the direst poverty of the imagination buy finery and indulge in extravagant moods in order to piece out their lack with other matter.

Aphorism, the expression of folk wisdom, is called upon to make sense of observations in the first piece, and the result is disjointed and incomplete as an "answer," but the reflection that follows takes another tack, celebrating the irrationality of human choice as an aspect of the imagination, a faculty that ordinary people may share with the greatest artists. There is no clear and definitive maxim; while the prose poems play off the tradition of the moral tale, the italicized text simply represents a greater reflective distance from the event, an "explanation" whose relation to the foregoing itself requires interpretation.[8]

As Williams' *Improvisations* show, the prose poem can be a democratic vehicle, incorporating the words and stories of ordinary people as well as those of the abject. We hear the voices of African-American Chicagoans in Fenton Johnson's prose poems, such as "African Nights":

> I am tired of work; I am tired of building up somebody else's civilization.
> Let us take a rest, M'Lissy Jane.

William Faulkner celebrates speech and stories from another locality in his *New Orleans Sketches:*

> Listen Baby, before I seen you it was like I was one of them ferry boats yonder crossing and crossing a dark river or something by myself; acrossing and acrossing and never getting nowhere and not knowing it and thinking I was all the time. You know — being full of lot of names of people and things with their own business, and thinking I was the berries all the time.

Such prose poems feed off and illuminate the beauty of local speech, its rhythms and images, from New Jersey to Chicago to New Orleans, and create a sense of place.

The sense of place extends to the literary and artistic "scene" as well: places like the café where Modernist writers and artists gather or just appear to be seen. But the effect is often ironic and derisive rather than celebratory. Poets in describing these scenes of eating, reading, observing and being observed explore and mock the hyper-self-consciousness of the individual playing the part of denizen of the literary sphere. In "At the Elite," Sanborn sketches a self savoring the act of reading Wyndham Lewis in the same way that he savors a raspberry cream, reducing the reading to a trivial delectation: "the savor of Wyndham Lewis melts down to the roots of my brain." Laura Riding is equally derisive in "In a Café" where the subject's self-conscious looking, rendered in a stream-of-consciousness prose, leads her to the thought that the imperfections of the place, such as the shade of brown in the curtains, are pleasing to her, putting her "in a sordid good-humour": "This attitude I find to be the only way in which I can defy my own intelligence. Otherwise I should become barbaric and be a modern artist and intelligently mind everything." Riding mocks the hypersensitive, elitist artist as a type, while the mocking subject also mocks her own pose, the silliness of staking her mood on the color of the curtains. Although the scene is less explicitly literary—an afternoon tea in a restaurant—T. S. Eliot's "Hysteria" belongs to the same genre of Modernist prose poem: a transcription of a moment through the hyper-conscious thoughts of an anxious self, here fearful of being swallowed by the laughing woman he faces, and fearful of the notice that they attract.

Describing more private scenes out of the public eye, the prose poem also affords a vehicle for the exploration of sexual themes, for Modernist flaunting of conventional mores and the insinuation of sexual acts and attitudes as text or subtext. Gertrude Stein's *Tender Buttons* often includes or encodes references to desire and lovemaking within seemingly detached observations of the instability of objects. For instance, in "A Substance In A Cushion," the sight of the cushion's clitoral "tassel" leads to the thought of "a violent kind of delightfulness." Harry Crosby's prose poems from *Sleeping Together* take the evocation of the details of desire and its violence as a central theme, as in "Embrace Me You Said":

> Embrace me you said but my arms were riveted to the most exacting of walls, embrace me you said but my mouth was sealed with the huge hot fruit of red wax, embrace me you said but my eyes were seared by the severities of two thousand winters—embrace me you said in such a low and feline voice that my eyes began to open like frightened shutters, in such a low and feline voice that my mouth became unsealed like red ice in a bowl of fire, in such a low and feline voice that my chains dropped like silver needles to the floor and my arms were free to encircle the white satin nudity of your voice which I tore into thin strips of music to store away in my heart whose desert had been threatened with vast armies of female laborers marching down dusty roads strewn with the prickly leaves of the cactus plant.

The poem relates a sequence of actions and emotions, beginning with restraint, even sexual inhibition, which is then released by the word, here characterized as a desiring catlike female voice. But once released, the libido emerges as violent and deadly, aiming to destroy and store the object of desire, literally the seductive voice, in a desert-like heart, the dusty receptacle of memory.

Crosby's prose poem may also be characterized as surreal; such prose poems portray the logic of dreams, their imagery and narratives, the scenery of the unconscious, formations of desire and horror. They feature volatile mixtures of body imagery, violence, and radical transformation. This strain recalls the role of Rimbaud both as an early and influential practitioner of the prose poem and a forerunner of Surrealism. In this volume, Paul Bowles' "No Village" begins on a Rimbaldian note, with flowers speaking: "What tentacles of clematis have been declared?" and goes on to depict a colorful apocalypse: "The ashes of dawn are in a million throats, and a thousand motors press upon the heart. Into the lavender crevices of evening the otters have been pushed, and slowly rises the one dark fume of the lake. Kill this unswerving figure. . . . On the earth all is laughter. Where have you led me, Astrea?" These figures as harbingers of a new but horror-filled beginning are reminiscent of the flowers that look, the beavers, Bluebeard, purple forest and speaking flower, Eucharis, of Rimbaud's "After the Deluge." Edouard Roditi's prose poems seem inspired not only by Rimbaud but also by Surrealist painting; for instance, the Magritte-like facelessness in Roditi's "Metamorphosis":

There were no more faces.

One day above the western gate of the city there appeared a grey cloud shaped like a hand. As the hand came nearer it was seen to hold a glove; and when the hand was above the city like a dark sun at its noon, the glove fell.

Immediately all faces disappeared. A man who was buying an umbrella first became aware of this; he raised his head and saw that the salesman's face had been replaced by a large oval green leaf. He looked at his own face in a mirror and saw that it had also been replaced by a large oval green leaf.

The alarm was given. Men ceased to disagree over this or that. The goldfish in the bowl in Mrs. X's drawing-room ceased to think that they were the centre of the universe. . . .

Although less identifiably surreal, in Kay Boyle's "Summer," we find a landscape that takes on the aspect of dying bodies, littered with embryonic cabbages: "August crops wrinkled with young cabbages deplanted and wilting in the new soil. Weight of the deflated flesh, the white-corded bellies, topples the spindle-stems. Blood, still as a snail's track, bulges the blue veins. There is an obscene chastity in the white potted skin. The white peak of the leaf presses the dark soil, rearing the white body upward." It is an imagery that borrows from the surreal to achieve its vividness in a horrific vision of rotting newness. The influence of Surrealism is found as well in works by one of the youngest poets in the collection, Mary Fabilli, an indication of the persistence of the surreal beyond the era of Modernism into the postmodern prose poem. In Fabilli's "They in Whose Dreams," for instance, we find dream images and dream logic in images of death and its transformations, evocations of fear, distant voices and music, and uncertain wandering: "They in whose dream no sanctuary dwells live by the ant-trails, follow their journeys on the kitchen floor. His voice from the bedroom drives down the road. Grieg from the radio. . . . She is dead already, lying in a pool of yellow wax."

Finally, the prominence of the apocalyptic and oneiric is a strong indication of a larger concern, the preoccupation with time, absence, memory, its loss and recovery that is distinctly Modernist. In Margaret Anderson's "Landscape," the image of "just before a storm, old sunken docks, boats and rocks on the bottom of great waters, [that] raise dark terrifying rejections of themselves to the too quiet surface" represents the momentary presence of the absent person through memory. Holly Beye writes of loss and the dream of willing the lost one's return through an imagined moan of "the time of your being away" in "For the Singer That Is Gone"; her "The Release of Hostages" records what is remembered of a grandfather, his "harsh shadow of a voice," and what has been lost: "Even when I shut my eyes and try very hard, I can't remember that man now." Such notes of loss, recovery and the instability of memory, whether the remembering is soothing or frightening, appear throughout the collection.

Despite or perhaps in conjunction with this elegiac thread, the Modernist prose poem owes a debt to Rimbaud in yet another way: as an affirmation of life, complexly represented. In the introduction to his recently published translation of Rimbaud's *Illuminations*, John Ashbery reminds us of what was "modern" about these now canonical texts which he places among the "masterpieces of world literature" (13):

[A]bsolute modernity was for him the acknowledging of the simultaneity of all of life, the condition that nourishes poetry at every second. The self is obsolete: In Rimbaud's famous formulation, "'I' is someone else" ("Je est un autre"). In the twentieth century, the coexisting, conflicting views of objects that the Cubist painters cultivated, the equalizing deployment of all notes of the scale in serial music, and the unhierarchical progressions of bodies in motion in the ballets of Merce Cunningham are three examples among many of this fertile destabilization. (16)

To this list, we may add the Modernist prose poem amply represented by the works included in this collection. These prose poems partake in an aesthetic that would depict the multiplicity of life from many angles in any given instant of time, including the impinging of the unconscious on the language of consciousness, of dream on diurnal experience. Jean-François Lyotard characterizes the modern (in order to conceptualize the postmodern) as that which "devotes its 'little technical expertise' (son 'petit technique'), as Diderot used to say, to present the fact that the unpresentable exists."[9] The Modernist prose poem's toolbox, its "petit technique" that includes the music of fused sentences, of simulated noise running over snatches of speech, of moments of dissolving syntax, brief revelations, and oneiric eruptions, provides synecdoches of the unpresentable, creating a sense that something else remains at the end of the reading.

1. Recent books revising our sense of what Modernism was, such as Robert Scholes' *Paradoxy of Modernism* and Michael North's *Reading 1922: A Return to the Scene of the Modern*, argue that critics should pay more attention to the middle ground of Modernism, as it were, as opposed to thinking in binaries, such as high art and pop culture, that Postmodernism itself challenged, parodied, and collapsed. So although I begin with Stein, who was among the most experimental of Modernist writers, deemed "extreme or geometric" by Scholes (59), *Family Portrait* includes a telling range of texts in terms of their difficulty and degree of audacity in breaking down conventional means of representation. Nonetheless, certain themes and preoccupations emerge repeatedly among these texts that we may also confidently link to the Modernist era.

2. Elsewhere I have argued that the prose poem suffered from its reputation as a Decadent genre for High Modernists like T.S. Eliot, a reputation buttressed by the notoriety of Oscar Wilde's "prose poem," a letter to Lord Alfred Douglas presented at his criminal trial, and the condemnation by Irving Babbitt, Eliot's professor at Harvard, of hybrid genres as "unmasculine" in *The New Laokoon: An Essay on the Confusion of the Arts* (Murphy 43–60). Steven Monte argues that other forms, e.g. free verse and especially the long poem, gave Modernists like Eliot and Wallace Stevens alternative vehicles for incorporating the prosaic into poetry (12–13; chapter 6), so the prose poem was less necessary to the Anglo-American Modernists than to the French. Regardless of its neglect by the best-known Modernists, the genre did provide a form conducive to Modernist experimentation in ways unlike other verse forms at the time.

3. Julia Nelsen also points to the affinity of the prose poem as an experimental form with the culture of the little magazines where many Modernist prose poems, including a number from this collection, first appeared: "The fact that it [the prose poem], too, stood at the margins of literature made the genre perfectly appropriate for experimentation within the laboratory of the little magazines, and drew poets to explore its untapped possibilities" (48).

4. Antoine Adam, notes, 972.

5. Lowell, "A Consideration of Modern Poetry," 114.

6. Cummings' verbal play and ebullient mix of description and bar speech may be characterized as nearly Joycean; it is worth noting that *Ulysses* began to appear in short chunks (resembling prose poems) in *The Little Review* in 1918; cummings' prose poem was published in 1925.

7. See Robert Alexander, "Contributors' Notes" for this volume.

8. James Longenbach would read the italicized passages of *Kora in Hell: Improvisations* as prose, not prose poetry, a "commentary [that] emphasizes narrative links that the prose poem suppresses" (97). But the "thematic perspicuity" (98) of the commentaries is not sustained; these commentaries strike me rather as the mental flights of a reflecting consciousness reaching for the stability of aphorism, a grasping for wisdom within the stream of experience. This riffing on the theme of the preceding improvisation is true to the title of the collection: it is an improvisation on an improvisation, but with the distancing effect of reflection.

9. "Answering the Question: What Is Postmodernism?" trans. Régis Durand in *The Postmodern Condition* 78.

Works Cited

Adam, Antoine, ed. *Oeuvres complètes.* By Arthur Rimbaud. Paris: Gallimard, 1972.

Alexander, Robert. "Contributors' Notes." *Family Portrait.*

Ashbery, John. Preface. *Illuminations.* By Arthur Rimbaud. New York: Norton, 2011.

Longenbach, James. *The Art of the Poetic Line.* St. Paul: Graywolf, 2008.

Lowell, Amy. "A Consideration of Modern Poetry." *The North American Review* 205.734 (January 1917): 103–117.

Lyotard, Jean-François. "Answering the Question: What Is Postmodernism?" Translated by Régis Durand. In *The Postmodern Condition: A Report on Knowledge.* Minneapolis: Univ. of Minnesota Press, 1984.

Monte, Steven. *Invisible Fences: Prose Poetry as a Genre in French and American Literature.* Lincoln: Univ. of Nebraska Press, 2000.

Murphy, Margueritte S. *A Tradition of Subversion: The Prose Poem in English from Wilde to Ashbery.* Amherst: Univ. of Massachusetts Press, 1992.

Nelsen, Julia. "Modernist Laboratories: The Prose Poem and the Little Magazines." *Letteratura e letterature* 4 (2010): 47–65.

North, Michael. *Reading 1922: A Return to the Scene of the Modern.* New York: Oxford Univ. Press, 1999.

Rimbaud, Arthur. *Illuminations.* Translated by John Ashbery. New York: Norton, 2011.

Scholes, Robert. *Paradoxy of Modernism.* New Haven: Yale Univ. Press, 2006.

Family Portrait

Virginia Admiral (1915–2000)

THE ESCAPED BEAR

Bright gray waves with white are beside us—we hurry, leaning along the beach, to reach the place before the great disaster. Our foreheads cut the wind leaving place for the bodies to follow. Then it comes toward us and we see that it is black and swirling through the sky covering the light and covering the sky. It is now unavoidable and cuts into our heads—it takes them off in a cold black grit.

There is a girl waiting with a crowd of people in a building—she holds with a big chain the tremendous bear—the chain is around his neck. The people look curiously—they have all come here to see the convicts lead the animals back for the night. On the upper floor I hold the bear with great anxiety but no fear. In a moment I see that he has taken the chain from his neck and slipped it into his mouth, this with great malevolence—he turns with the chain in his mouth and looks at the people. They do not realize that, if he can do this, in another moment he will be free to slip it off and run wild. They look at him with curiosity still and at me—but I am responsible. If he is free so am I—but only free to escape. Now I am a fugitive.

Another girl sits behind a polished counter—she answers questions to sailors and has books for the insurance company and the government. She is a secretary with great authority and is responsible for the convicts. I have been here once but now it is written in her books that I have escaped because the bear did and that I have caused the bear to escape and do great damage never repaired. She sees me now and I have let my hair stay up but part of it straggles down, hoping to disguise myself—my clothes are wrinkled and I look wild. But she recognizes my disguise and now they know what I have done and will look everywhere to find me and take me back to worse than before. I am sitting in a street-car and I see this escaped girl come in—she sits beside me and I recognize her—I tell her we will go back to the place where we lived and hide her. We go there and it is the first floor of an old office building with sheets hung up to cover the display windows. The spirit of the secretary is filling this place. The woman inside is cooking and when she knows me she says, "If that is so, we will put one less light bulb in the cooking pots—and we will keep them behind these curtains with only the cord coming out to the outlet. Then they will not see that we are cooking." But everyone knows anyway and we cannot hide here. The spirit of the secretary and all of the people watching are here in this place and it will not be very long before they are really here.

Margaret Anderson (1886–1973)

OCEAN AQUARIUM

I do not love nature but I give great attention and respect to the elements. I am not pleasant about things that are on-the-make or reproductive. The elements belong to eternity and are a communication. When it rains I pause in my life and say to myself "it rains and all the unforgotten rains are raining."

Tonight the wind from the Atlantic blows until outside there is only wind. I follow it back to its beginning at the middle of the ocean . . . The fish and sea-flowers and sponges have withdrawn to a position behind the wind and there I can watch the fish swimming up and down making a glistening wall of light, rolling their eyes and flashing their fins at the empty water left to the winds. And I know if the sea were uninhabited man would have died of his terror of an empty sea.

LANDSCAPE

Water-oats that marked and hid the river are dead now . . . all night wild ducks and water birds make their wooden noises. At evening the sea-meadows and the river show corrupt and silent colors. Today the sun through an ocean gale and ocean clouds poured steady parallels of light into the heavy sunken bay: a holy picture where some one stronger than Jesus might walk.

This is the bay.

There are a lot of houses in the town. She must have lived in one of them. But that does not matter . . .

She told me that she used to come here . . . cross this bay to the ocean beyond everyday in her white boat. I did not know her then, I do not know her now. She has even long ago left her description . . . but this is the bay.

I have seen in northern places, just before a storm, old sunken docks, boats and rocks on the bottom of great waters, raise dark terrifying rejections of themselves to the too quiet surface.

I watch the bay in all weathers. There is upon it in the nights a pale white reflection: a nerve-chart of tiny routes made by a white boat.

IMAGISM

Sea orchards and lilac on the water, and color dragged up from the sand; drenched grasses, and early roses, and wind-harps in the cedar trees; flame-flowers, and the sliding rain; frail sea-birds, and blue still rocks, and bright winds treading the sunlight; silver hail-stones, and the scattering of gold crocus petals; blackbirds in the grass, and fountains in the rain; lily shadows, and green cold waves, and the rose-fingered moon; pine cones, and yellow grasses, and a restless green rout of stars; cloud whirls, and the pace of winds; trees on the hill, and the far ecstasy of burning noons; lotus pools, and the gold petal of the moon; night-born poppies, and the silence of beauty, and the perfume of invisible roses; white winds and cold sea ripples; blossom spray, and narcissus petals on the black earth; little silver birds, and blue and gold-veined hyacinths; river pools of sky, and grains of sand as clear as wine. . . .

. . . dream-colored wings, and whispers among the flowering rushes; of moonlit tree-tops, and the gaiety of flowers; brown fading hills, and the moving mist; sea rose, and the light upon the poplars; shaken dew, and the haunts of the sun, and white sea-gulls above the waves; bright butterflies in the corn, and a dust of emerald and gold; broken leaves, and the rose and white flag-stones; sea iris with petals like shells, and the scent of lilacs heavy with stillness; scarlet nasturtiums, and dry reeds that shiver in the grasses; slim colorless poppies, and the sweet salt camphor flowers; gold and blue and mauve, and a white rose of flame; pointed pines, and orange-colored rose leaves; sunshine slipping through young green, and the flaring moon through the oak leaves; wet dawns, and a blue flower of the evening; butterflies over green meadows, and deep blue seas of air, and hyacinths hidden in a far valley. . . .

. . . harsh rose and iris-flowers painted blue; white waters, and the winds of the upper air; green wine held up in the sun, and rigid myrrhbuds scented and stinging; the lisp of reeds, and the loose ripples of meadow grasses; mists on the mountains, and clear frost on the grass blade; frail-headed poppies, and sea-grass tangled with shore-grass; the humming brightness of the air, and the sky darting through like blue rain; strewn petals on restless water, and pale green glacier-rivers; somber pools, and sun-drenched slopes; autumn's gold and spring's green; red pine-trunks, and bird cries in hollow trees; cool spaces filled with shadow, and white hammocks in the sun; green glimmer of apples in an orchard, and hawthorn odorous with blossom; lamps in a wash of rain, and the desperate sun that struggles through sea mist; lavender water, and faded stars; many-foamed ways, and the blue and buoyant air; grey-green fastnesses of the great deeps; a cream moon on bare black trees; wet leaves, and the dust that drifts over the court-yard; moon-paint on colorless house.

. . . Pagan temples and old blue Chinese gardens; old pagodas glittering across green trees, and the ivory of silence; vast dark trees that flow like blue veils of tears into the water; little almond trees that the frost has hurt, and bitter purple willows; fruit dropping through the thick air, and wine in heavy craters painted black and red; purple and gold and sable, and a gauze of misted silver; blue death-mountains, and yellow pulse-beats in the darkness; naked lightnings, and boats in the gloom; strange fish, and golden sorceries; red-purple grapes, and Assyrian wine; fruits from Arcadia, and incense to Poseidon; swallow-blue halls, and a chamber under Lycia's coast; stars swimming like goldfish, and the sword of the moonlight; torn lanterns that flutter, and an endless procession of lamps; sleepy temples, and strange skies, and pilgrims of autumn; tired shepherds with lanterns, and the fire of the great moon; the lowest pine branch drawn across the disk of the sun; Phoenecian stuffs and silks that are outspread; the gods garlanded in wisteria; white grave goddesses, and loves in Phryggia; wounds of light, and terrible rituals, and temples soothed by the sun to ruin; the valley of Aetna, and the Doric singing. . . .

. . . The moon dragging the flood tide, and an old sorrow that has put out the sun; whirling laughter, and the thunder of horses plunging; old tumults, and the gloom of dreams; strong loneliness, and the hollow where pain was; the rich laughter of the forest, and the bitter sea; the earth that receives the slanting rain; lost treasure, and the violent gloom of night; all proud things, and the light of thy beauty. . . . Souls of blood, and hearts aching with wonder; the kindness of people—country folk and sailors and fishermen; all the roots of the earth, and a perpetual sea. . . .

TOWARD REVOLUTION

On Thanksgiving Day some five thousand men and women marched in Joe Hillstrom's funeral. Why didn't they march for Joe Hillstrom before he was shot, everybody is asking.

Yes, naturally. Why not?

Incidentally, why didn't someone shoot the governor of Utah before he could shoot Joe Hill? It might have awakened Capital— *and Labor.* Or why didn't five hundred of the five thousand get Joe Hill out of jail? It could have been done. Or why didn't fifty of the five thousand make a protest that would set the nation gasping?

There are Schmidt and Caplan. Why doesn't someone see to it that they are released? Labor *could* do it. And there are the Chicago garment strikers. Why doesn't someone arrange for the beating-up of the police squad? That would make a good beginning. Or set fire to some of the factories, or start a convincing sabotage in the shops?

Why aren't these things done?

For the same reason that men continue to support institutions they no longer believe in; that women continue to live with men they no longer love; that youth continues to submit to age it no longer respects; for the same reason that you are a slave when you want to be free, or a nonentity when you would like to have a personality.

It is a matter of Spirit. Spirit can do anything. It is the only thing in the world that can.

For God's sake, why doesn't someone start the Revolution?

Sherwood Anderson (1876–1941)

THE CORNFIELDS

I am pregnant with song. My body aches but do not betray me. I will sing songs and hide them away. I will tear them into bits and throw them in the street. The streets of my city are full of dark holes. I will hide my songs in the holes of the streets.

In the darkness of the night I awoke and the bands that bind me were broken. I was determined to bring old things into the land of the new. A sacred vessel I found and ran with it into the fields, into the long fields where the corn rustles.

All of the people of my time were bound with chains. They had forgotten the long fields and the standing corn. They had forgotten the west winds.

Into the cities my people had gathered. They had become dizzy with words. Words had choked them. They could not breathe.

On my knees I crawled before my people. I debased myself. The excretions of their bodies I took for my food. Into the ground I went and my body died. I emerged in the corn, in the long corn-fields. My head arose and was touched by the west wind. The light of old things, of beautiful old things, awoke in me. In the cornfields the sacred vessel is set up.

I will renew in my people the worship of gods. I will set up for a king before them. A king shall arise before my people. The sacred vessel shall be filled with the sweet oil of the corn.

The flesh of my body is become good. With your white teeth you may bite me. My arm that was withered has become strong. In the quiet night streets of my city old things are awake.

I awoke and the bands that bind me were broken. I was determined to bring love into the hearts of my people. The sacred vessel was put into my hands and I ran with it into the fields. In the long cornfields the sacred vessel is set up.

SONG OF THE SOUL OF CHICAGO

On the bridges, on the bridges—swooping and rising, whirling and circling—back to the bridges, always the bridges.

I'll talk forever—I'm damned if I'll sing. Don't you see that mine is not a singing people? We're just a lot of muddy things caught up by the stream. You can't fool us. Don't we know ourselves?

Here we are, out here in Chicago. You think we're not humble? You're a liar. We are like the sewerage of our town, swept up stream by a kind of mechanical triumph—that's what we are.

On the bridges, on the bridges—wagons and motors, horses and men—not flying, just tearing along and swearing.

By God we'll love each other or die trying. We'll get to understanding too. In some grim way our own song shall work through.

We'll stay down in the muddy depths of our stream—we will. There can't any poet come out here and sit on the shaky rail of our ugly bridges and sing us into paradise.

We're finding out—that's what I want to say. We'll get at our own thing out here or die for it. We're going down, numberless thousands of us, into ugly oblivion. We know that.

But say, bards, you keep off our bridges. Keep out of our dreams, dreamers. We want to give this democracy thing they talk so big about a whirl. We want to see if we are any good out here, we Americans from all over hell. That's what we want.

THE LAME ONE

At night when there are no lights my city is a man who arises from a bed to stare into darkness.

In the daytime my city is the son of a dreamer. He has become the companion of thieves and prostitutes. He has denied his father.

My city is a thin old man who lives in a rooming house in a dirty street. He wears false teeth that have become loose and make a sharp clicking noise when he eats. He cannot find himself a woman and indulges in self-abuse. He picks cigar ends out of the gutter.

My city lives in the roofs of houses, in the eaves. A woman came to my city and he threw her far down out of the eaves on a pile of stones. Nobody knew. Those who live in my city declare she fell.

There is an angry man whose wife is unfaithful. He is my city. My city is in his hair, in his eyes. When he breathes his breath is the breath of my city.

There are many cities standing in rows. There are cities that sleep, cities that stand in the mud of a swamp.
I have come here to my city.
I have walked with my city.
I have limped slowly forward at night with my city.

My city is very strange. It is tired and nervous. My city has become a woman whose mother is ill. She creeps in the hallway of a house and listens in the darkness at the door of a room.

I cannot tell what my city is like.
My city is a kiss from the feverish lips of many tired people.
My city is a murmur of voices coming out of a pit.

SISTER

The young artist is a woman, and at evening she comes to talk to me in my room. She is my sister, but long ago she has forgotten that and I have forgotten.

Neither my sister nor I live in our father's house, and among all my brothers and sisters I am conscious only of her. The others have positions in the city and in the evening go home to the house where my sister and I once lived. My father is old and his hands tremble. He is not concerned about me, but my sister who lives alone in a room in a house on North Dearborn Street has caused him much unhappiness.

Into my room in the evening comes my sister and sits upon a low couch by the door. She sits cross-legged and smokes cigarettes. When she comes it is always the same—she is embarrassed and I am embarrassed.

Since she has been a small girl my sister has always been very strange. When she was quite young she was awkward and boyish and tore her clothes climbing trees. It was after that her strangeness began to be noticed. Day after day she would slip away from the house and go to walk in the streets. She became a devout student and made such rapid strides in her classes that my mother—who to tell the truth is fat and uninteresting—spent the days worrying. My sister, she declared, would end by having brain fever.

When my sister was fifteen years old she announced to the family that she was about to take a lover. I was away from home at the time, on one of the wandering trips that have always been a passion with me.

My sister came into the house, where the family were seated at the table, and, standing by the door, said she had decided to spend the night with a boy of sixteen who was the son of a neighbor.

The neighbor boy knew nothing of my sister's intentions. He was at home from college, a tall, quiet, blue-eyed fellow, with his mind set upon football. To my family my sister explained that she would go to the boy and tell him of her desires. Her eyes flashed and she stamped with her foot upon the floor.

My father whipped my sister. Taking her by the arm he led her into the stable at the back of the house. He whipped her with a long black whip that always stood upright in the whip-socket of the carriage in which, on Sundays, my mother and father drove about the streets of our suburb. After the whipping my father was ill.

I am wondering how I know so intimately all the details of the whipping of my sister. Neither my father nor my sister have told me of it. Perhaps sometime, as I sat dreaming in a chair, my mother gossiped of the whipping. It would be like her to do that, and it is a trick of my mind never to remember her figure in connection with the things she has told me.

After the whipping in the stable my sister was quite changed. The family sat tense and quiet at the table and when she came into the house she laughed and went upstairs to her own room. She was very quiet and well-behaved for several years and when she was twenty-one inherited some money and went to live alone in the house on North Dearborn Street. I have a feeling that the walls of our house told me the story of the whipping. I could never live in the house afterwards and came away at once to this room where I am now and where my sister comes to visit me. And so there is my sister in my room and we are embarrassed. I do not look at her but turn my back and begin writing furiously. Presently she is on the arm of my chair with her arm about my neck.

I am the world and my sister is the young artist in the world. I am afraid the world will destroy her. So furious is my love of her that the touch of her hand makes me tremble. My sister would not write as I am now writing. How strange it would seem to see her engaged in anything of the kind. She would never give the slightest bit of advice to any one. If you were dying and her advice would save you she would say nothing.

My sister is the most wonderful artist in the world, but when she is with me I do not remember that. When she has talked of her adventures, up from the chair I spring and go ranting about the room. I am half blind with anger, thinking perhaps that strange, furtive looking youth, with whom I saw her walking yesterday in the streets, has had her in his arms. The flesh of my sister is sacred to me. If anything were to happen to her body I think I should kill myself in sheer madness.

In the evening after my sister is gone I do not try to work anymore. I pull my couch to the opening by the window and lie down. It is then a little that I begin to understand my sister. She is the artist right to adventure in the world, to be destroyed in the adventure, if that be necessary, and I, on my couch, am the worker in the world, blinking up at the stars that can be seen from my window when my couch is properly arranged.

Holly Beye (1922–2011)

FOR THE SINGER THAT IS GONE

On the roof, the rain chatters like the cold one under the bridge. Since five o'clock I have watched for the evening star above the cypress trees but now I know it will not come.

When on the stones outside the door, fleeing footsteps make a hollow sound, I know before they have passed they are not yours. Where do the little sparrows find warmth on such a night?

I have put the fire on. I have made a pot of strong tea and cut thick slices of bread. But enclosed in the veil of the nightrain from far off comes the sharp sour smell of the acacia, the golden acacia, the shower of sunfire enchanting us and closing us round with its unapparent darknesses. Then I think of smiles whose meaning was not clear, disorder in familiar households, promises dishonored and foresworn, the recurrence of violent transformation.

And there is no comfort in the soft wind.

Oh you who departed falsely, the time of your being away rushes like the rain into the gutters of the street. If you could hear the spectral moan of it as it is born away never to return and having no use in its fury, and could you feel again the quiet within, would it not then come to you a hundred different ways by which you might return?

IN THE EUCALYPTUS FOREST

Who were we when we walked through the Eucalyptus forest, in the tall silence, through the thick quiet of our walking?

You can stretch your full height and they are still far above you, where the sun's keen edge washes the wings of the jay, where the bats have secret nests.

If they are tall and straight in their columns, and the light cutting like wind across their rough soft-silvery coats seems to push them toward the edge of the cliff, what is it in the distant homeland calls them back?

Then why did we cry in the silence of our footsteps, in the rustle of that soft glad longing in us once again?

Who has been long in that other place where the shadow of the murderer is gray on every face and all night long the hammers of that terror intrude their surgery upon the one who sleeps, will know why we stayed till the evening star rose over the hill.

And why we cried in the Eucalyptus forest for the ones we had left behind.

FACES IN A FURIOUS NIGHT

Because they no longer had anything left to say to one another and yet were reluctant to put a notice of foreclosure to their friendship, they met at the very door of the movie house and went inside at once, putting off until intermission, when once more they would be left side by side with that long, hostile silence between them, the diversion of buying popcorn, gum and those faded-green passion flowers, to which all movie-goers at least become addicted.

THE UNREMITTING STAIN

Does your blood run cold at this thought: that you, standing knee-deep in that eighteen years' October night, with your kisses on the stranger's mouth teaching fire to the stars, now O destroyed dear curled-leaf girl, like wintered grasses hilltop the barren winds. . . Shall never again the antlered rider open his cloak to your underworlded remorses? Stay you no longer the graying river witches! There stand—beheld by the bringers of death in the broad, vast-flung undesiring. The screech-wheeled elevators to thy sunken marriages, the doom-eyed many harkenings after the dear Lord knows why, O blot up these crafts of the brindled irretriever. . . That sang you the world's communion in the hand of the stranger on thee. . . For its great laugh wet with tears. . . For the marvelous Christmases spinning themselves through that red, swept current. For the ghostly iron bells crossing above mist-swept fields behind the towers of unworthy kings and storms and hesitations. Where hand-in-hand overthrew the telephoned-cold and a mother's greed. Laughed that wild bastard joy against the poised teeth and the darkening wind. . .

Sweet gold of thy strawberry hours, to old-men honors never again persuaded, nor mill-ground in stinking sanctity, behold it now—those angry hands, to whom thy young belly rounded, wringing themselves and crying out over the field where ghostly lovers walk!

THE RELEASE OF HOSTAGES

My grandfather, wearing patent-leather shoes with pointed toes and leaning heavily on his ebony cane, stood in the doorway.

"Put the light on!" said his harsh shadow of a voice, filling the hallway with an oppressive musty odor. "It's dark for an old man here!"

It was July.

Outside, in the humid twilight, birds retuning to their nests twittered in busy conversation like Chinese women leaving some dingy factory together. A pink peony blossom, snatched from a neighbor's bush, lay across the doorstep, its crushed petals sending into the house an intoxicating fragrance.

"Put the lights on, somebody. . . !" he kept calling, knocking his cane sharply against the iron doorstop.

Even when I shut my eyes and try very hard, I can't remember that man now. For the life of me, I couldn't tell you whether or not his eyes were blue, if his skin tended to the ruddy, if he carried a gold pocket watch and chain, nor even if there were three black whiskers on his ears, which may have been large and nearly perpendicular to his head.

But so it may have been. For just now when a red truck rattled past the house, loaded to the top and dangling from either sides a load of chimney brooms, the morning air was suddenly full of the sound of nesting birds, and for one long, exquisite moment, the smell of peonies against a darkened doorstep. . .

SOME NEW KNOTCHES WITH AN OLD KNIFE

Of such parts was my Aunt Ebony that each time the doctor came at her summons, he left feeling worse than he ever had before.

"Why'nt you treat things as they are, Boy, 'stead of as how you allow they shouldn't be!" she'd cackle up in the rafters of someone's plaintive draft.

"Come off it, now! Come off it!" He'd like to be sharp, but that's a problem when you're dealing with Old Eb, an unqualified boomerang artist.

"How's about it, Dr. J? One for the road?" Always a sucker for an old lady's wheedle, he lets himself be persuaded every time to take one of those four-horsepower nebutals he always keeps handy for in- and out-patients on his route.

And then, of course, it was all fun and frolic for her, scampering from bush to bush all up and down the roadside bracken, slingshotting his bubblegum tires with raspberry thorns in the pitchy blackness, where better than anyone the two of them knew as how Jet and Ebony were not the only species born as a consequence of lightning bugs.

Paul Bowles (1910–1999)

from NO VILLAGE

I

What tentacles of clematis have been declared? The ashes of dawn are in a million throats, and a thousand motors press upon the heart. Into the lavender crevices of evening the otters have been pushed, and slowly rises the one dark fume of the lake. Kill this unswerving figure. Into what green halls has it been led? Under what long hills has it smothered softly during the night? In the dark the yards at the edge of the jungle are hot. Panthers move dankly on wet leaves and the breath of the trees falls heavily in festoons of fetid mist. On the earth all is laughter. Where have you led me, Astrea? Are the hills always as remote as they are this night? Is every lane as cold as your finger? There will be no more declarations. There can be no hour uncounted. The floor of the garden will heave silently and in the sea nearby there will be a great explosion. Lava from the beaches will congeal to form starfish and all the universe will be submerged in a sea of fire-coral. Seawrack will twist to choke the throats of poets and the moon rising from behind the lagoon of phosphorus will blind the armadillos. Each crystal hill will shiver into a home for octopi. I shall hear no more the drip of whaleblood on the floor of the cabin. The wind in the trees will linger but a while. All the fronds of the climbing vines at the pane will shrivel to shrill music and the ants will perform a subterranean adagio. No hands will celebrate the ritual with mystery.

II

Carrion in the noon field, shame the vultures. They have awakened me from sleep. Flies that hum in sedge beneath the linden, there is no retreat. There is no more conversation. The fruit in the meadow is drying in the drought, and the brook that whispers somewhere under the witchgrass moves but seldom. Mud, rise from your limestone bed in the gulley, come to me, smear me with coolth. Mountains that flock on the far horizon, camels of the eastern plains, chase no more the long cirrus. Over the ashtrees listen no longer to the laughter of starflowers.

IV

Now the sun will reach this rock, but the music of the glen will remain a monotone between the cliffs. You have brought me deep into this place and no one remains here but two souls. The sun cooks the hemlock needles above the shale and your hand, your hand lies on the bank, nearing the sunlight. Leeches writhe anchored to the streambed and your arms already shine silver in the sun. And ever more distinctly the one tone of the glen is heard, heard now below the cliffs. Soon the sun will shade patterns on your shoulders, on your back. The sheen of your back will blind the birds above and the sun will race across the sky to the night. Slowly we shall leave behind the sound of continuous water, forgetting that we have existed. The ferns will scatter clouds of spores and a harmony of quiet will burst from our warm lips. Do you doubt? The sun knows your hair, and wild raspberries fall down the bank at my feet. The glen hums and a dragonfly disappears. Where in the forest could I see a yellow bird were it not for your watchful eyes? When could I spot savory mushrooms pushing from old leaves and dry needles had you not a delicate sense? Had I not you, of what avail would be the path to the glen? The sallow late sky shrieks as a locomotive crawls across the canyon. Three lizards hurry to hide beneath flat stones and you move your arm out of the pale sunlight. Jewelweed bursts to remind the landscape of cows plashing in pastures after rain. A toad squats by a stone and milkweed down sails over our heads. You have brought me deep into this place and there is no retreat. Even at night there will be no respite. The monotone of water traveling on circular clouds under pebbles will continue; the water will rush.

VIII

Astrea, I shall tell you the final place where the eyes will rest. The lemontrees line the harbor and the sharktooth is buried in the foam. The noonday sand glitters and sailors enter the squalid cafés. The whistle of a steamboat beyond the promontory is an ague and the redhaired woman eats a tangerine. The yellow pennant shakes in the seawind and the butcher on the sidestreet eats his lunch. In the park the swans croak and barnacles are scraped from the ship's side. The narrow streets shudder with heat as the cactus on the hillside hides the scorpion. The mechanical piano vomits a sour melody. In the patio the fountain dribbles. Stretch, cape, sixteen miles away, and stop the larger tropic waves. The octopus is languid in the aquarium and the lizards run along the gravel by the roses. On the quay the beggar dozes and horses stamp hungrily in the square. The day lunges into the hot afternoon and the wind shrills angrily across the beach. The lighthouse stands a white obelisk and urchins bathe by the causeway at the edge of the town. The girl sobs in the courtyard. Two raging cats rack the air with cries. The wheels on the cobblestones make a presto and from the hill the mountainrange is topped with snow. And in the lazy valley there is no village.

Kay Boyle (1902–1992)

SUMMER

I

Flying curved to the wind shearwaters turn their bodies in the wave. Sea hisses under the weed-hair, ice-armored foam plucked to vermillion bubbles by the beak of the wind. Rocks crouch under the gold hill where cypresses groove darkly like a negro lying down in wheat.

II

I press through the enclosing darkness to the window. Sky is torn sharp as steel on the yucca horns, clouds pierced tight as whorls on the yucca horns, plaques of firm flame-black on black embracing darkness that curve up to sleek and handsome yucca horns.
Hysteria of the trees is palpable through the closed window and the wall. The dry tongue of my sheet turns me slowly, tentatively.

III

Wind, tendinous, drifting dark and subtle in the channel, indolent, with one arm stroking the shore. Reeds follow the movement, flowing to light, following the mystery of muscles liberated under flesh.

Wind, fingering the rain and the melon-flowers. . . the black-horned fungus growing under rye.

IV

August crops wrinkled with young cabbages deplanted and wilting in the new soil. Weight of the deflated flesh, the white-corded bellies, topples the spindle-stems. Blood, still as a snail's track, bulges the blue veins. There is an obscene chastity in the white potted skin. The white peak of the leaf presses the dark soil, rearing the white body upward.

V
LABOR HORSES

Stones draw sharp threads of blood across your hoofs. Whips pry upon your hooded silence, men's voices shrill at the unshaken core.

The young mare passing, preens her petaled throat, thin nostrils cupping quivering globes of flame. Tongues lolling below sagged withers, fumble an old response. No glittering coil, drawn like a miracle, unfurls no strong sweet rings of flame. The empty-caverned loins open parched mouths, gape wearily away. . .

Your eyes are wounds, your bones old weapons rotting in the flesh.

VI

BEFORE STORM

Firm palm of the sky curved above the roofs and the sharp river; dark unshaken palm above the yellow fire of mustard-weed and the savage sunflowers pacing across the dust. The palm is closed. The fields twist in their scarlet ribs, the valleys quiver in shadow, the wagonroads flutter like white ribbons from the proud dark wrist. . . the palm curved dark and imminent, unopened. . .

VII

MONASTERY

Petalless vines of light stain the window with tendrils. Walls stretch their bleached dark—fibred limbs across the hill.
On the blue lake in his hair, his palms, white-throated, fold their wings and linger. Evening shuffles in as he walks, breaking radiant foliage on the sunset, bearing great bunches of rich black and seedless grape.

VIII

WHORE STREET

Street bruised blue from the nudge of the wind, artery clogged with the setting sun. A white curtain trembles like a blade undrawn from the quick. Bed, baring firm iron limbs, scars the approach of darkness.
Breasts swing in slow delirious rhythm, caressing the odors that

73

twitch unslaked in the gutter. Eyes press upon the withered man-
darin of sun.

The night resmoothes his hair. . . memory dangling hot tongues. . .
behind his eyes the white ripe fruit, the wine that crouches at the
core. . . a white arm lifted, odor from the pit staining the sagging
mattress of the sea.

JANUARY 1, U.S.A.

Annie-Lou, the prettiest girl in Seattle, was unable to speak intelligently on many subjects. "We're really awfully lucky to be alive now," she said. "It's such a wonderful time. It's so recently that they've made eye-black that doesn't run and kiss-proof lipstick and permanent waves." In the night club the ballet was stepping wild "La Nuit de Légalité," the violins lisping, the basses snoring the name of the man who sprang from the winds in full flight. He was not Nijinsky, being of Seattle, of no old splendor. He was the picture of a rainbow in spite of his jowls and the gold crowns on his teeth. After him came a group of male dancers with violets for modesty, pansies for thoughts, daisies for simplicity on their brows. Even their neat, grey moustaches and their bald heads did not mar the perfection of the whole. They tossed gilt-edged cards in a shower over the tables. This, the wild extravaganza comparable to "Une Nuit de Cléopatre" but modernly unlike it, inspired by the words "New Deal," and bringing the businessman into play. One small viola, almost a violin, dressed in a Schiaparelli oil-cloth frock and under the influence of legal liquor, climbed on a table and wailed: "He asked me to marry him, not to marry him, but to marry him, if you know what I mean." Legally, legally, legally, sobbed the cellos, and the dancers, sobbing, took the measure. But it was no more than a catch in the throat, having been composed not for poverty but for prosperity, words by Beatrice Fairfax, clothes by Mrs. Fellowes, mental appeal by George M. Cohan. "It's a New Deal, you mustn't squeal, you'll get a meal," tinkled the triangles. Annie-Lou lifted her perfect features from the table where they had fallen and gulped: "Tomorrow I can look Daddy in the eye and say sure, I was drunk again last night, but it was legal, sweetheart."

JANUARY 24, New York

I

In one corner of the dormitory, near the roof, was a pigeon-cote in which more than fifty birds were cooing. The chief prisoner was a pigeon-fancier, the warden said with an apologetic smile. The detectives shifted their cigars in their mouths and looked wearily around the room. "Why, he's so soft-hearted he has to leave the building when the cook's killing one of the birds for his supper," the warden went on. "You know what he's in for?" snapped the commissioner. "Burglary, felonious assault, and homicide."

II

The detectives went through the first tier of cells in the west wing, throwing out everything they found. The prisoners were driven out and they huddled at the end of the flats, some of them rouged, their eyebrows painted, two holding blankets around their naked shoulders. Out from the cells sailed corsets, compacts, perfume bottles, a blonde wig, nightgowns, high-heeled slippers and ladies' underwear. The detectives went up to the second tier and herded the prisoners out. "I wouldn't work here for a thousand berries a week," a detective said. "I'm just not that kind of a girl."

III

The commissioner remarked that such characteristics were common in prison, but that it was disgusting to see them flaunted in this way. He didn't think he'd ever get over the shame of what he'd seen. The kingpin had a great weakness for lemonade, said the warden with an indulgent smile. The detectives pried open the locker in his cell: it was filled with tinned peaches, olives, pickled herrings, malted milk, copies of *The New Yorker,* and a deck of heroin. "If you lay a finger on my rosary," said the kingpin in a high falsetto, "I warn you I'll scream."

from FOR AN AMERICAN

—for e. w.

I

You are the scorched columns, the green nave which struck thirteen times by lightning continues to thrust mon chevalier Saint Michel into the clouds. Below you, the windows are pleated in the Roman stone: blades of green grass hung with fine moss and delicate bouquets of lichen. . . .

You have danced with your hard feet backward, as an Indian dances, through the dry stalks and the silver milkpods which tapped at the cups of your knees; over burnt ground and devastation, through bush of bloodless berry where no other vegetation could survive; over soil closed like a fist about the roots of flowers; over violence and dry rot; under grapes gone to powder in their fine skins.

Not plumes of the sea did you offer, but gaunt feathers, bare rigging of ships, desert foliage, wind like metal in the nostrils, wind dark, rich, sweet in the mouth.

Who shall say I have not known you if I have set with the pillars of the church growing about me, air thin as glass and stones like firm lids upon my eyes? I have seen the bronze statue seven times larger than a sheep above the refectory whose windows open like a silk fan, and the black saint reeling with clouds, dripping with vines of fresh rain.

I have seen the candles lit at the altar's prow, so simple that the carving became a desecration; and the shadows of the church rising and breaking on pure cones of candle-foam . . .

and you like a candle lit at the extremity of the ermine sleeve: a bright wing in the night, a flame bleached out in the sun.

II

There is no wilderness in America to salvage. None with the tough bark of the trees as black, and the flowers solid and sweet between the teeth. Nowhere else does flesh become to the eye as odor in the nostril.

Under the stripped trees the earth of this country lies in strong furrows. The tongue of the plow carves avenues of loam. Spring nineteen-twenty-six and the soft bodies of moles lying like small black panthers in the trail of the horses' feet. Only here is the earth among the roots of the trees printed with toad feet, needled with moss, dark and inseparable about the fine bones of the fern.

There is this then to set between the bitter cold and the summer. This to return to and discover like new leaves at that season: spring, and his hair falling two ways on his forehead; tassels of fresh rain, and his mouth.

Emily Holmes Coleman (1899–1974)

THE WREN'S NEST

When over the highway and through the brush a tramp on the wind came lightlysighing then into the lane down the trodden periwinkles shuddering between forced stones fled the captive and after her the futile trailing of her long red skirt. She sang up to the wren's nests and built for herself on the stone wall a house of bark and silence.

His eyes were waterfalls over the rocks and from his chin went out assurance of desire. They had come together on the hill where the cows went astray and he had seen her with her long branched stick chasing them back into the valley. She jumped on the back of one and it ran sinking to the stream. Down to the stream they had gone and their feet had chiseled its depth. They stood making rivulets through the dam and lay on the bank in the sun with his hat over her eyes and his arm across her breast. The cows wandered up the hill again and in the stinking sun they lashed the great flies and chewed their contemplation beneath the trees.

Come on with me. We must while them home now and you can meet my mother. His hair wet from the stream had dried, and in the slumber of summer his ears and cheeks had gone wet and his hair above his ears was coiled in small turnings. I cannot stand that, she said to him, come with me and put on your hat. I have to go back to the city he told her.

In the evening she sat out on the porch and listened for the whippoorwills. He had shyly eaten their supper and afterwards bidden her mother a courteous goodbye. He had fastened her hand to his breast outside and gone gleaming down the dust to the village where the trains left for the large cities.

A nice young man, her mother called, come back in here why dont you, its cooler in here. She went in and sat in the dusk by the cold stove. If only you hadnt married said her mother you might have had him just think of it. I dont care she said I dont want him. She took her mothers hands and sang softly to her cap.

Well thats all there is to romance said her father at the breakfast table when the syrup glued out of the pot and from up the round soft bakings came flavor of buckwheat and sun.

*   *   *

In after years when the early winter winds pinched the trees and made of red and gold a barren silence she put on a coat of blue and caught up her skirt in the mirror. All there is for me to do is to walk like this and it can be done. Her hat fitted snugly and the feather was bright red. You will come back said her mother you will find that the cows cannot go alone.

You see that he doesnt let them wander in the sun said she deftly and pressing finely her mothers face. You will all be quiet and when I return there will be mourning. Into the buggy she stepped primly and waved a small white handkerchief to her mother on the porch. Go inside you will catch something there because the wind is coming.

The train screamed on frenzied wings through the green and out over the water and in again to trees. She sat with her bag above her head and her knees folded over. The woman across the aisle lived in many places and had come from Europe that day. She gave her a little pin of violet to look in and see the European cities. If she would not like me I could think my thoughts. In the brown meadows, touched with green, there were cows. They melted into the green and stood sighing beneath the trees.

She went out to the platform and stood alone from the woman and sped across the earth. Little houses of brick and sand muttered in the corners and fast through the afternoon went the train and fast into the night. Over the gulleys and swift into the sun and rattling across the iron bridges over the towns. It was coming fast, fast from the little houses, closer to the train and faster to the trees. It shattered and swung and lifted and rocked and fast into the city went the train. It was coming, it would be the end and she would stand alone and motionless upon the track. Are you coming? And the fast bled trees stood off their dull response.

Now into the city went the train and hushed from her eyes and bent her head. And crushed across the narrow streets on iron structure and poured hot fire into the shed at the end. This was the city he was shouting and the baggage was piled at the end. She leaped from her ears and quieted her hands with sorrow. She was to stand upon the curb and see people going to their places and speaking a foreign tongue.

*   *   *

What do you think you can do here you had better go home and speak your piece. I dont care I shall stay anyway. It was with fervor and soft hands pressed against the glass.

You dont seem to realize he told her that anything so exquisite belongs in the sun and shade. Not here she said there is no sun. They sat drinking in a cold cafe and on the ground were sparrows jumping for the cheese. There were woodchucks and little wrens. All on the stone wall. Will you go to market in the morning and tell me what you find? No she said I am afraid you will be gone.

That settles it he said I will not have my will abrogated. She laughed against the frown on his white and famished brow.

So what more there is to do is hard to say. If you will consult your husband you may find that there is cause for your return. But I love your hair she said it flows over your head and you are not a boy. Go back he said it was not meant for you.

* * *

My mother can see that I have come back. Green in the damp and weltered in the marsh. For the apples I was gone, the apples sunk into the kettle and mashed. They were good in the jars. Thank you my mother your hair is of course not wet like his and silk and cold. But where is your husband she told her, you did not see him. Oh yes many things we talked and he has learned to love me. Then why didnt you bring him with you? I found him cold and interested in many vices.

Crowded into the memories of the winter came the spring, warm in the swamps and drying. She sat along the stone walls with her stick and pushed them into ponds for her desire. Will you go back from me she fiercely shouted to the sun and went violently up the lane behind him. She struck from her hand the stick and made pools in the mud of love and vengeance. She built cities in the wood and crossed twigs over their depths and sang. Now chocolate for the horses of the Tsar they will be calling for them. She hitched golden horses to the old carriage of her impotence and they stood champing and did not run away. Over the bars it would come and out rattling to the highway, dragged behind him. She went softly up behind the bull and poked him with her stick. He leaned to one side and nosed in the ground. She poked him again on his white and listless flank and he sprang quivering on his feet and turned to poise his head. Into the ground went bellowing his clotted hoof, pawing not grimly and leaning to one side. Under his head all fury and design and lurching to her his trembling legs. She advanced an inch and poked his light nostril and stood lilting to the fence. Down with his snorting went the wind and over to her place went fury belching bull head in restraint and tail high on the wind. Close to her smell came bent and perching head and over the fence went she with grace of flouting spring. He came up short where she had leaped and backed and belched and gouged upon the bars his sharp tined horns made havoc in the logs.

Enough for you she cried with pointed stick go back lie down under the sun and gouge again the pails made of cardboard.

Harry Crosby (1898–1929)

from SLEEPING TOGETHER

EMBRACE ME YOU SAID

Embrace me you said but my arms were riveted to the most exacting of walls, embrace me you said but my mouth was sealed with the huge hot fruit of red wax, embrace me you said but my eyes were seared by the severities of two thousand winters—embrace me you said in such a low and feline voice that my eyes began to open like frightened shutters, in such a low and feline voice that my mouth became unsealed like red ice in a bowl of fire, in such a low and feline voice that my chains dropped like silver needles to the floor and my arms were free to encircle the white satin nudity of your voice which I tore into thin strips of music to store away in my heart whose desert had been threatened with vast armies of female laborers marching down dusty roads strewn with the prickly leaves of the cactus plant.

MOSQUITO

Let us go to our friend the mosquito and ask him if he will transfer one little crimson corpuscle from you to me one little crimson corpuscle from me to you in order to effect a mystic communication which will make our two hearts one. In exchange for his services we can offer to shelter him from the wind, in exchange for his services we can offer to steep him in liquid honey, in exchange for his services we can rescue him from the snare of the spiderweb. So that I was not astonished when I woke up to find that we were covered with mosquito bites for we had forgotten the white netting (we were in Venice) but in spite of having the mosquito at my mercy (he was too drowsy-drunk to fly away) I preferred to let him live and instead wreaked my vengeance on a swarm of wasps that infested our breakfast table.

OVID'S FLEA

The arching of your neck, the curve of your thigh, the hollow under your arm, the posture of your body, are more than anodynes throughout the length of my dream but although I have the power to be bright and wild I am baffled in my desire for absolute possession and I am forced to compare myself to Ovid's flea who could creep into every corner of a wench but could in no wise endanger her virginity.

I HAD NO IDEA WHAT THEY WOULD DO NEXT

I think it began by my pouring the coffee into the sugar bowl while you sitting up in bed with a mirror in your hand were humming your impossible melodies. I knew too that as soon as the sugar melted the white rain would begin to beat against the window. Outside a tree was dying at its roots but I was much more fascinated by the whiteness of your hands for I had no idea what they would do next. There seemed to be an inner light with sugar-squares of shadow outside and I seemed to be awaiting a reply in your eyes which I did not receive until I woke up and found them looking into mine.

IN SEARCH OF THE YOUNG WIZARD

I have invited our little seamstress to take her thread and needle and sew our two mouths together. I have asked the village blacksmith to forge golden chains to tie our ankles together. I have gathered all the gay ribbons in the world to wind around and around and around and around and around and around again around our two waists. I have arranged with the coiffeur for your hair to be made to grow into mine and my hair to be made to grow into yours. I have persuaded (not without bribery) the world's most famous Eskimo sealing-wax maker to perform the delicate operation of sealing us together so that I am warm in your depths, but though we hunt for him all night and though we hear various reports of his existence we can never find the young wizard who is able so they say to graft the soul of a girl to the soul of her lover so that not even the sharp scissors of the Fates can ever sever them apart.

HUMAN FLESH AND GOLDEN APPLES

Like the horses of Diomedes I am being nourished with human flesh while you are eating the golden apples of the Hesperides. I suppose they are the apples of the Hesperides for they are so very big and gold. There is a clean sound of gravel being raked. The shadows under your eyes are blue as incense. Your voice is the distant crying of night-birds, your body is the long white neck of the peacock as she comes down the gravel path. Your mouth is an acre of desire so much as may be kissed in a day, our love the putting together of parts of an equation, so that when they knocked on the door at nine o'clock I could not believe that you were in the country and I alone in a hotel in New York forced to take consolation in the bottle of white rum that I bought last night from the elevator boy.

WHITE CLOVER

There is a clairvoyance of white clover, a coming towards me of the white star-fish of your feet, an aeolus of drapery. Your hand on the knob of the door is the timidity of the new moon, your hair over your shoulders a cataract of unloosened stars, your slender arms the white sails you lift to the mast of my neck. Not even the silkiness of new-drawn milk can compare to your skin, not even the cool curves of amphora can compare to the cool curves of your breasts, not even the epithalamiumic gestures of an Iscult can compare to your queenliness. Your ears are the littlest birds for the arrows of my voice, your lap the innocent resting place for the hands of my desire. And as you sit nude and shy on the edge of our bed I wonder at the miracle of the opening of your eyes.

GOLDEN SPOON

Your body is the golden spoon by means of which I eat your soul. I do not seek to find the explanation for this curious sensation which is more visual than tactile. But I am afraid of the army of silver spoons marshaled in array under their commander-in-chief Silver Fork who is about to give a command to march against the golden spoon which I hold desperately in my mouth.

WHITE SLIPPER

A white aeroplane whiter than the word Yes falls like a slipper from the sky. You come dancing over the silver thorns of the lawn and by holding up the corners of your rose-and-white skirt you catch the white slipper which I kick down to you from the sun.

e. e. cummings (1894–1962)

from POST IMPRESSIONS

VIII

i was sitting in mcsorley's.   outside it was New York and beau-
tifully snowing.

Inside snug and evil.   the slobbering walls filthily push witless
creases of screaming warmth chuck pillows are noise funnily swal-
lows swallowing revolvingly pompous a the swallowed mottle with
smooth or a but of rapidly goes gobs the and of flecks of and a
chatter sobbings intersect with which distinct disks of graceful
oath, upsoarings the break on   ceiling-flatness

the Bar.tinking luscious jigs dint of ripe silver with warmlyish wet-
flat splurging smells waltz the glush of squirting taps plus slush of
foam knocked off and a faint piddle-of-drops she says I ploc spit-
tle what the lands thaz me kid in no sir hopping sawdust you kiddo
he's a palping wreaths of badly Yep cigars who jim him why gluey
grins topple together eyes pout gestures stickily point made glints
squinting who's a wink bum-nothing and money fuzzily mouths
take big wobbly foot-steps every goggle cent of it get out ears drib-
bles soft right old feller belch the chap hic summore eh chuckles
skulch. . . .

and i was sitting in the din thinking drinking the ale, which never lets you grow old blinking at the low ceiling my being pleasantly was punctuated by the always retchings of a worthless lamp.

when With a minute terrif   iceffort one dirty squeal of soiling light yanKing from bushy obscurity a bald greenish fetal head established It suddenly upon the huge neck around whose unwashed sonorous muscle the filth of a collar hung gently.

(splattered) by this instant of semiluminous nausea A vast word-less nondescript genie of trunk trickled firmly in to one exactly-mutilated ghost of a chair,

a;domeshaped interval of complete plasticity, shoulders, sprouted the extraordinary arms through an angle of ridiculous velocity commenting upon an unclean table.and, whose distended immense Both paws slowly loved a dinted mug

gone Darkness   it was so near to me, i ask of shadow won't you have a drink?

(the eternal perpetual question)

Inside snugandevil.   i was sitting in mcsorley's
It, did not answer.

outside.(it was New York and beautifully,snowing. . . .

from PORTRAITS

IX

at the ferocious phenomenon of 5 o'clock i find myself gently decomposing in the mouth of New York. Between its supple financial teeth deliriously sprouting from complacent gums, a morsel prettily wanders buoyed on the murderous saliva of industry. the morsel is i.

Vast cheeks enclose me.

a gigantic uvula with imperceptible gesticulations threatens the tubular downward blackness occasionally from which detaching itself bumps clumsily into the throat A meticulous vulgarity:

a sodden fastidious normal explosion; a square murmur, a winsome flatulence—

In the soft midst of the tongue sits the Woolworth building a serene pastile-shaped insipid kinesis or frail swooping lozenge. a ruglike sentience whose papillae expertly drink the docile perpendicular taste of this squirming cube of undiminished silence, supports while devouring the firm tumult of exquisitely insecure sharp algebraic music. For the first time in sorting from this vast nonchalant inward walk of volume the flat minute gallop of careful hugeness i am conjugated by the sensual mysticism of entire vertical being, i am skillfully construed by a delicately experimenting colossus whose irrefutable spiral antics involve me with the soothings of plastic hypnotism   . i am accurately parsed by this gorgeous rush of upward lips. . . .

cleverly

perching on the sudden extremity of one immense tooth myself surveys safely the complete important profane frantic inconsequential gastronomic mystery of mysteries
                    , life.

Far below myself the lunging leer of horizontal large distinct ecstasy wags and. rages Laughters jostle grins nudge smiles push—.deep into the edgeless gloaming gladness hammers incessant putrid spikes of madness (at

Myself's height these various innocent ferocities are superseded by the sole prostituted ferocity of silence, it is) still 5 o'clock

I stare only always into the tremendous canyon the , tremendous canyon always only exhales a climbing dark exact walloping human noise of digestible millions whose rich slovenly obscene procession always floats through the thin amorous enormous only lips of the evening

        And it is 5 o'clock

        in the oblong air, from which a singular ribbon of common sunset is hanging,

snow speaks slowly

Harriet Dean (1892–1964)

DEBUTANTE

You are a faded shawl about the shoulders of your mother. A puff of wind catches at your fluttering edge to jerk you away. But she draws you close, growing cold in the warm young breeze. She holds you with her shiny round pin, as all young ones are clasped to old by round things grown shiny with age.

In your wistful tired eyes I see the trembling of her shawl as she breathes.

BARN-YARDING

I cannot joyously write little things. Perhaps that is why I write none at all. The little people about me fill me with disgust. They are cocksure bantam hens, loose and fertile, laying egg-thoughts carelessly. The crack of shells is loud, but tiny wet chicks roll out, smaller than the rest. God forbid that I am of the same breed! If I must linger in the barn-yard for a few days, studying the swagger of these hens and silently measuring my own, may I in the end fly away to my mountain-top—alone in the night. Strut, if I must, but quite alone.

Their voices are splinters of sound which prick my desolation to shreds. My one great fear is that clumsily they may stumble against my loneliness. What matter if the tongue be unknown to me! These tone arrows beat at my door like undesired rain; they hurl themselves against my tissue walls until I shall go mad with their urgence.

The only true friendliness near me is the blank brick wall of the house next door. I wrap myself in its unresponsiveness and stop up my ears with its cold silence that I may have courage to go on with my work.

Flame curtains flap in my grate and send grey indistinctness shivering and stumbling over my walls.

A dusty mirror in a lonely house waits. . . .

DEPARTURE

"And now you, too, must go," she said to me; I who had already gone, silently, tenderly lest my steps break the stairs of her heart.

H. D. (1886–1961)

from FOUR PROSE CHORUSES

2.

Strophe.

. . . I love you would have no application for the moment. I love you waits with cold wings furled; stands a cold angel shut up like cherry-buds; cherry-buds not yet half in blossom. The cold rain and the mist and the scent of wet grass is in the unpronounceable words, I love you.

. . . I love you would have no possible application. It would tear down the walls of the city and abstract right and grace from the frozen image that might have right and grace pained upon its collar bones. The Image has no right decoration for the moment, is swathed in foreign and barbaric garment, is smothered out in the odd garments of its strange and outlandish disproportion.

. . . the Nordic image that stands and is cold and has that high mark of queen-grace upon its Nordic forehead is dying . . . is dying . . . it is dying, its buds are infolded. If once the light of the sheer beauty of the Initiate could strike its feature, it would glow like rare Syrian gold; the workmanship of the East would have to be astonishingly summoned to invent new pattern of palm branch, new decoration of pine-bud and the cone of the Nordic pine that the Eastern workman would so appropriately display twined with the Idaian myrtle. The Idaian myrtle would be shot with the enamel of the myrtle-blue that alone among workmen, the Idaian workmen fashioned in glass and in porphyry, stained to fit separate occasion and the right and perfect slicing of the rose-quartz from the Egyptian quarry.

. . . the Nordic Image is my Image and alone of all Images I would make it suitable so that the South should not laugh, so that the West should be stricken, so that the East should fall down, bearing its scented baskets of spice-pink and little roses.

Antistrophe.

. . . flowers fall, unreasonable, out of space and counter point of time beaten by the metronome of year and year, century on century. The metronome is wound up, will go on, go on beating for our life span; a metronome tick of year, year, year; life for life; heart beat on heart beat, beats the metronome holding us to the music that is the solid rhythm of the scale of the one, two, three, four; one, two, three, four, I am here, you are there; tell me I am here and I will tell you, you are there; but the metronome ticks a metronome music and the voice flinging its challenge to all music in the teeth of Reason stays for no tick, tick; the heart that springs to the feet of Love with all unreason, stays no moment to listen to the human tick and tick of the human metronome heart-beat.

. . . heart you are beating, heart you are beating, I am afraid to measure my heart beat by your heart beat for I am afraid with the shame of a child struck across fingers by the master that says play soft, play loud, play one-two-three-four again, again. I am struck across the fingers and across the mouth. My mouth aches with the unutterable insult of one-two-three-four.

. . . O, friend or enemy. Why can't I cry out, fall at your feet or you at my feet, one or the other overcome by the beauty of the metronome whose beauty is unassailable, or overwhelmed, overcome by the fragrance, dripped, ripped, sputtered, spread or spilt!

Epode.

. . . voiceless, without a voice, seeking areas of consciousness without you. Seeking with you areas of consciousness that without you would no more be plausible. Set up choros against acted drama, the high boot, the gilt wreath of ivy for some dramatic deity; set him forth, crown him with pasteboard pomegranates . . . pasteboard pomegranates have nothing to do with this reality. Out of the air, into the air, the color flames and there is pulse of thyme, fire-blue that leads me across a slab of white-hot marble. My feet burn there and the wet garment clings so that I am a nymph risen from white water. So you over-seeing, burn into my flesh until my bones are burnt through and attacking the marrow of my singular bone-structure, you light the flame that makes me cry toward Delphi. Were pasteboard pomegranates of any worth or plums stitched on to a paper crown? Listen . . . men recounted your valor, shut you up in strophes, collected you in pages whose singular letters are still laced across your spirit. The Greek letters are an arabesque shutting you in, away, away; you are shut in from the eyes that read Greek letters. Take away the gold and manifest chryselephantine of your manifest decoration and you are left . . . seeping into wine-vats, creeping under closed doors, lying beside me . . .

Strophe.

. . . Love stands outside. Love is wrapt away has nothing to do with painted images, Ionic painted images and dolls set before old shrines. Before an old shrine are dolls' eyes painted edgewise and a masculine doll with one side-eye painted in cobalt and eye-lash in black hematite. One male doll stands edgewise with male outline and the male chest is parallel slant. One eye is painted edgewise and the eye-lid is black cobalt.

. . . sing of the painted images set before a shrine under the Idaian snows. Sing of the vermilion that paints the centre of the male god image, the little straight vermilion thread that is *the lips are a line of scarlet O my love, thy thighs are pomegranates.* No ripe pomegranate but the straight masculine chastity that bids chastity stand upright. Sing of the vermilion thread that is the scarlet thread of the sandal-strap painted with feet set straight and pointed toward the other . . .

Antistrophe.

. . . sing of the other with painted pleats to the transparencies that are the straight pleats of its revealing garment. The feminine doll stands facing us kneeling in the Idaian dust, the shrine by the road-side that stands before the wilderness of the wild-orange and the blossoming oleander. The oleander in this place is rose-rosette of painted cornice of an old treasure house at the edge of the line of inhabited streets leading to the temple. Oleander is a rosette set here, there in old-fashioned regularity among the architraves of an outgrown and discarded fashion. Sing of the oleander, a flat flower and little given to perfume. Sing of the wild-orange not to be sculptured on the temple but copied in little flat wire pattern to be placed, flat and wire, filigree about the forehead of an image.

   . . . sing of Love for there is no fashion and no pattern that may reveal him set upright with rose and red and blue fading from immortal images set upright.

Epode.

   . . . sing of Beauty, there is no song yet reveals it. Sing of beauty that is Masculine, that is Feminine that stands a monster before Delphi. Sing of beauty that cried only to God only for there is no counter-beauty to mate Beauty.

   . . . Sing of Beauty set before the tracks, set at each curve of the race-track. Sing of the fleet sons of the North and the dark sons of the South and the grey-eyes ivory-thighed sons of the West and of the sons of the East who were eyes matched in perfect glass-hematite contour. Sing of the four corners of the earth for 4 is the second sacred number of the Delphic sun-god placed at every shrine and before every open door of the initiate.

   . . . Sing of beauty that may not be sung ever. Sing of the straight parallel of Beauty that sings only to itself, self-revealed among the initiate in the white corridors of every academy and of every ancient temple. Sing of Beauty, self-revealing for no one reveals the beauty that itself is in itself all-revealed. Sing of the white flame of the white sun-God Helios whose beauty is unnamed even among the initiates. Sing of the Beauty of Love set upright with no blue and no red and no old-blue painted in fadeless color. Sing of the One God set upright whose agile flame burns the color of the red-tulip from the wings of the Idaian God set upright, sing of the Love, the white lightening to the sun-image, without which the sun—image and his manifest number the secondary 4 of the inviolate nations was without meaning to the initiate.

. . . sing of love never revealed save to the initiate.

Robert Duncan (1919–1988)

AT HOME

Since we have had the telephone removed, the interrupted spirits of the household have begun again, or we hear again their story telling. In these counsels of objects, animals and ourselves, these concentrations and exfoliations of language, we have our source. When silence blooms in the house, all the paraphernalia of our existence shed the twitterings of value and reappear as heraldic devices.

There was a solitary purpose all the time, the undistracted gaze of the bee that lives for honey—a hum that we waited to hear. In this device we picture the rose, thornd; the bee, barbd; the hive, an armd citadel of sweetness.

The second device is a cloud dispersed, a falling apartness in itself having no other images. Below this: clouds drifting, in which images emerge. The cloud is perhaps idleness, is a being without lineaments, a mereness of metaphor that is not sensible. This figure in writing is the poetry of Gertrude Stein. In which are all the pleasures and pains of reading with none of the rewards and values. This is what we IMAGINE her to have done. Below is the actual procession of clouds we watch where meanings appear and disappear.

The third device is a cat dreaming, which we see as dearness of nearness. His paws stretcht out so that the toes branch show he is almost awake in dreaming. He has been carelessly, confidently, cast down in sleep, so that we know he knows we are here. This cat has been drawn often by us, so, posing without imposing, curld in a chair or as if nesting in himself anywhere about.

The fourth device is a tree among trees, that is, a forest which is the conversation in silence we are referring to. The tree recalls also the Ace of Spades which is a death among deaths, that is, a solitude which is the house we live in and in which our love is stored.

The fifth device is a bear dancing, muzzled or not as the designer chooses, but this means an ancient allegiance exists between joy and the kin. The sixth, the moon, which I see as the intellect as it waxes and wanes, drawing and releasing the tides of a sea we do not picture in hearing. We had only to distinguish what we belongd to from what we did not belong to to cast off all busyness and return to the work which I speak of here as a honeycomb composed of inscrutable pictures, a shield of discrete poems which may absorb or cast back all meanings, remaining undisturbd. Hence our love of René Magritte. For his paintings resemble the cells of such bees.

CORRESPONDENCES

It is from the ideas of you that you emerge. I return to you from my longing, you a second image in longing, drawn to you as the painter is drawn to the man he draws; or, as in reading the cards, one is drawn to the likeness of death in the Ace of Spades. "I say I shan't live five years" Blake wrote in 1793 "And if I live one it will be a Wonder." Within all daily love—and this is a world—is another world sleeping or an otherness awake in which I am a sleeper. The reveald things of this order appear as omens: within the full dread of death, so that I cry up to die—is another life. I tremble lest the door be lockd or open, for the door is an ununderstandable joy.

But now, across an emptiness of time I see you. I shall never reach you—between me and thee.

As it was in the beginning. What I am withdraws from the great sun, like a lion retracting his roar in order to speak. In this scene the simple pleasures of this world cause areas of torment in the unreal like stones in an open field.

SOURCE

Or: I work at the language as a spring of water works at the rock, to find a course, and so, blindly. In this I am not a maker of things, but, if maker, a maker of a way. For the way in itself. It is well enuf to speak of water's having its destination in the sea, and so to picture almost a knowing in the course; but the sea is only the end of ways—could the stream find a further course, it would go on. And vast as the language is, it is no end but a resistance thru which a poem might move—as it flows or dances or puddles in time—making it up in its going along and yet going only as it breaks the resistance of the language.

When I was about twelve—I suppose about the age of Narcissus—I fell in love with a mountain stream. There, most intensely for a summer, staring into its limpid cold rush, I knew the fullest pain of longing. To be of it, entirely, to be out of my being and enter the Other clear impossible element. The imagination, old shape—shifter, stretcht itself painfully to comprehend the beloved form.

Then all windings and pools, all rushings on, constant inconstancy, all streams out of springs we do not know where, all rush of senses and intellect thru time of being—lifts me up; as if out of the pulse of my bloody flesh, the gasp of breath upon breath (like a fish out of water) there were another continuum, an even-purling stream, crystal and deep, down there, but a flow of waters.

I write this only to explain some of the old ache of longing that revives when I apprehend again the currents of language—rushing upon their way, or in pools, vacant energies below meaning, hidden to our purposes. Often, reading or writing, the fullest pain returns, and I see or hear or almost know a pure element of clearness, an utter movement, an absolute rush along its own way, that makes of even the words under my pen a foreign element that I may crave— as for kingdom or salvation or freedom—but never know.

UNKINGD BY AFFECTION

One exchanges the empire of one's desires for the anarchy of pleasures. But pleasures themselves, one finds, are not domestic, and the troubles of the soul cast jewel-like reflections upon the daily surfaces. One has moved only to a world where the devoted household common places cast shadows that are empires; where the warmth of the hearth is kept alive in a cold that extends infinitely, the dream of a king ruthless in his omnipotence, a plenitude of powers, an overreaching inspired pretention, an *unam sanctum*, a papal conceit over all beloved things.

We live within ourselves then, like honest woodsmen within a tyrannical forest, a magical element. Sheltered by our imaginary humble lives from the eternal storm of our rage.

CONCERNING THE MAZE

We were surrounded at that time by avenues of escape. You began at a certain point and went on, and the streets were the natural runways where we tried the same turn over and over again being lost in the maze. Where only a second before someone had passed before us we could smell fear and confusion in their sweat along the walls.

One of us got a dry section of cheese by running the right angle and then twice to the left. He tried it again and found the same dry section of cheese. One ran down past three bypaths, turned the circle, went down instead of up and found a hole gnawed in the wood. He went through, out into the world on the other side of the sky. Others have crouched at that crack in the wall entangled in wire, pissing with fear, seeing only the glassy reflection of their own eyes on the other side.

*   *   *

If we always had found food there, and then there was no food, if then there is never any food there where we had expected to find food: there are definite somatic results that such a frustration has on us. We lose sleep. Our hair grows thick with secretions and coarse and scarce with age. Our skin is scaly. And we are given to tremens.

It is even more horrible when we can find no doors.

We kept seeing that there was a certain way to get at the food. It was very simple. We could all see that—that it must be very simple, a very very simple thing, an everyday thing that any one of us could do. There were only a given number of things among which we could choose: jump onto the little platform, roll the wooden ball down the groove, turn to the right and pull the latch, run up the inclined plane and jump into the net, make a dive for the door at the far corner of the room. But only one of these was the correct choice. Any one thing, if it were wrong, would set into motion a cycle of events which might never lead us back to an opportunity, back to the GREAT OPPORTUNITY which we now faced. It was very simple, however. It was OBVIOUS that one of these things—maybe rolling the wooden ball down the groove—would bring freedom. It was surely a very commonplace thing, some one of these simple acts that any of us, as I have said before, could do to release himself. Some of us had made the choice before and run wild to come again and again to this same place, but we could not remember what we had chosen—the trials that had resulted from that choice had been so severe. I only want to tell something about the choice. It is a simple thing to jump onto the platform and find out, to roll the wooden ball down the groove and find out, to run up the inclined plane and jump and find out, to turn to the right and release the latch and find out, to make a dash for the door and find out. But we remember the ordeals of the years that come from a wrong choice, and we have returned here so many times that we cannot remember what choices we have made that were wrong. It seems as if all of them are wrong, and yet we know that that is not so. There is one right way. There is only that way, we know that there is a way we have not tried before, one which will save us, but we have gone thru so many errors that we cannot be sure that any given act might not be a repeated error.

It is so simple. A choice among five acts. Yet some have died of exhaustion. And it is hunger not over-eating that gives us nightmares.

*　*　*

Parables are partly true.

*　*　*

There was a long narrow tunnel or a hall cut into a great block of stone with barely enough room for two to pass if they stood sideways against the walls, and I was running on a treadmill there. Far down the hall I could see a man standing in the white light of a doorway. There was a fire inside the room behind him of burning newspaper, never consumed. I could see this man standing, and I was conscious that I was very young and that the treadmill would go on forever. I remembered the horses, white and gawdy with ribbons that raced on the yellow treadmill in the circus. I raced on and on. L'idée fixe. I raced on and on. I could see this man standing, peering down the hall at me, miles down the hall; a great white light was all around him so that he stood black in the center of a white light that ran out like water over the sand of the floor, and I could hear all around us the terrific breathing of the sea. I noticed that the walls at my side were moist and salty. A coating of mucous surrounded me, loading me down as I struggled to move down the hall, my hoofs kicking out over the treadmill. The man standing at the door so far away couldn't see who I was. If I could only come near enough for him to recognize me, the problem of the foodtrap would be solved. At that moment I realized that the tunnel was under water. There was a rusty puddle all about me, and the treadmill had become clogged with sand and rubbish of shells and weeds washed in by the tides. I ran on and on down the long tunnel, knowing that I would drown when I reached the light.

T. S. Eliot (1888–1965)

HYSTERIA

As she laughed I was aware of becoming involved in her laughter and being part of it, until her teeth were only accidental stars with a talent for squad-drill. I was drawn in by short gasps, inhaled at each momentary recovery, lost finally in the dark caverns of her throat, bruised by the ripple of unseen muscles. An elderly waiter with trembling hands was hurriedly spreading a pink and white checked cloth over the rusty green table, saying: "If the lady and gentleman wish to take their tea in the garden, if the lady and gentleman wish to take their tea in the garden . . ." I decided that if the shaking of her breasts could be stopped, some of the fragments of the afternoon might be collected, and I concentrated my attention with careful subtlety to this end.

THE ENGINE

I

The engine hammered and hummed. Flat faces of American businessmen lay along the tiers of chairs in one plane, broken only by the salient of a brown cigar and the red angle of a six-penny magazine. The machine was hard, deliberate, and alert; having chosen with motives and ends unknown to cut through the fog it pursued its course; the life of the deck stirred and was silent like a restless scale on the smooth surface. The machine was certain and sufficient as a rose bush, indifferently justifying the aimless parasite.

II

After the engine stopped, I lay in bed listening while the wash subsided and the scuffle of feet died out. The music ceased, but a mouth organ from the steerage picked up the tune. I switched on the light, only to see on the wall a spider taut as a drumhead, the life of endless geological periods concentrated into a small spot of intense apathy at my feet "And if the ship goes down" I thought drowsily "he is prepared and will somehow persist, for he is very old. But the flat faces . . ." I tried to assemble these nebulae into one pattern. Failing, I roused myself to hear the machine recommence, and then the music, and the feet upon the deck.

Mary Fabilli (1914–2011)

THE MORNING LED

The morning led her sheep into the dim cold valleys. The wan light flowed like a sea over the dark ridges and deep black shadows. The house was cold, cold and sad as the whistle of the railroad train hurtling in the muffled distance towards the unknown windings of a sleepless night. How cold how sad the world was, the sheep bleating in her mind, and the tinkling of broken bells against her broken slumbers.

She drew the paper dolls from her heart and set them on the window sill, where they fluttered and whispered in the morning wind. She tore open her heart with a pair of scissors and let the gentle sheep walk out back to their home in the valley between low hills, near the high mountains humped up in power and silence under the grey eastern light.

She leaned on her elbows and watched the dead pavements and walls of the city, the hungry look of its vacant caves, while the morning wind freshened in the tinkling valleys. The serpent of the city, huge and soundless, writhed through the empty streets shedding a poisonous lustre, coiled nearer and nearer to her window without a sound. His huge convulsive ripples kept her attention fixed. Even after he had devoured her and moved on like a fog, she saw him winding nearer and nearer shedding his horrible lustre.

But the sheep were safe in the uninhabited valleys. There always mountains would watch over them, and morning would lead them into morning, from the dim cold regions of death to the sheltered sun-bathed meadows. She held her paper dolls out of the window, and let them drop from her fingers. They fluttered at last to the ground. She leaned over to watch them as they waved back helplessly, tiny and shrunken, from the bottomless depths of the city.

THEY IN WHOSE DREAMS

They in whose dreams no sanctuary dwells live by the ant-trails, follow their journeys on the kitchen floor. His voice from the bedroom drives down the road. Grieg from the radio. This night

this closed shell fearful of awakening clasped in a silent consciousness is more than by the walls of this room, the sound of the violin, or his sleepy watchfulness upstairs. This is a careful taking of ruin and a ruined skeleton, of remembering how her nose combined with her upperlip and her dyed blonde hair fell on a blunt and ruthless shoulder turned to exclude the other from the conversation. She is dead already, lying in a pool of yellow wax. Her dead eyes are ugly and her nose is crushed against her mouth. The pools of the world suck her under, and the land is turned to English moors where Emily walks following the turn of the wind.

They bend too as the winds bend, dreamers, whose mouths are bruised by their impassioned words. As the fog rolls over the stony city, and the siren calls, they raise their heads from the pillow and undulate in dreams and whisperings of savage soundlessness over the hideous caves and walls.

She was a criminal of vast importance, plating her hair with the sacred films of the sun. She stood before the tomb of life and threw javelins inside herself, and greedily she swallowed life, and killed herself and ate herself. The glutted light fell from her hair with brazen laughter. Her thick long fingers shriveled the gentle grass, and a river of black and ponderous gasses flowed from where she sat.

No sanctuary dwells by the ant-trails, or where music swells in the midnight room. The plated blondes are numberless and their insistent cunning devours the city and city-dwellers, flashes before the face of the sun blinding all but the dreamers.   But whose death is revealed to them—they have become powerless by their dreaming, by their long waiting for secret and midnight visitations. They drift in piteous waves over the caves of the darkening city, gentle, and merciful and unavailing.

THIS IS THE DAY OF FREEDOM

This is the day of freedom. This is the day of light. We have brought no flowers to our younger sister. She enters alone in a dark house running to look in all the corners to see if anything has changed. A year and a day and all things pass away. Sometimes they do not pass away. The small china ashtray with the blue decoration is eternal, it shall sit eternally on the little walnut table near the armchair. No change shall shatter the mirror near a corner of the room. Today is yesterday a million years ago. Behind the reflection in the mirror is a dark gloom, full of the darknesses of the past even to the beginning of childhood. All at once the white bare corridors of a dream seem better than this a thousand times, she turns quickly to rush away, but the doors and the walls and ceilings are barred with loving and wary smiles, are ribboned with the waving lips of kindness, and the arms and the lips and smiles bar her from the whitewashed dream.

This is a narrow house, this is a narrow room. I can touch the walls with my shoulders. The ceiling crowds down on my head. I have been here once before when the space was a little wider. It has grown smaller in my absence, and the streetcar tracks run down the middle of the floor. You must listen for the sound of the streetcar always, and be prepared to run out into the hallway among the sour smell of clothes and fog and crowded people.

Her mother and father and brother are standing in the canvas of the unusual pale grey frame. They are three tiny figures in the background, coming to her from a great distance but never advancing. The parallel lines of perspective move swiftly back from the foreground of the canvas and gather to a point at their feet. She watches them in amazement, and they gesture to her to sit down and take off her hat and coat. They are powerless to touch her. She begins to edge away from them along the wall of the room; they move quickly and spin like little black bobbins, but they cannot come nearer at all, they will never have the power to leave that position where the parallel lines have met. Finally she reaches the door, opens it, steps out an instant and slams it violently behind her. She is still in the room, and leaning with her back against the door facing the canvas, but she is out of the room, she is free of the room and of those little black people.

There are thousands of huge panes of glass shifting between herself and the canvas, noiselessly shifting to right and left unevenly. They had evidently always been there to save her from the disaster of touching those people, but she has never known this—she had never seen before the thousands of panes of glass shifting in noiseless erratic motion one after another. She began to take off her hat and coat, and walked to the window. She saw a streetcar rumbling by, and people walking to and fro quietly in the grey evening fog. Suddenly a million electric lights went on and the street opposite was packed with motion picture palaces from one end to the other as far as eye could see.

POEM

We who in a dream discount the horses whose broken hooves resound in the corridors of our narrow times, we who in a dream wax melody, we in ecstasy demand the equation, the simple simon of our way of life.

Come the divine hooves thundering on the hilltop, striking the smooth white pebbles and flinging aside the plants of Indian Paintbrush on the wayside, comes the delectable thunder on the paths of clouds, on the wings of stranded butterflies.

For the Capitol hill and the columns are crumbled and fallen; the pink clouds of evening cast lavender shadows on the fluted lines of those fallen columns. The old man with the crooked jaw stands under the broken arch and leans on the shoulder of the little black-amoor who is trussed up in ragged finery and embroidered satin. Doves perch on his fingers and ants crawl under the arch of his foot making a long line through the halls of this hungry ruin.

The horses crop the dried grass, tossing their white manes, stepping softly over the grounded magnolia blossoms. Their wings are furious with silence; the walls of the temple are deep-carved with denying words; the ants creep up the face of the wall and lose themselves in the troughs of the incised commandments.

This is the vision, white and black against the eastern sky. Knowing well the light diminishing; the long evening dragging slowly into night's consuming fire.

William Faulkner (1897–1962)

THE PRIEST

Evening like a nun shod with silence, evening like a girl slipping along the wall to meet her lover. . . . The twilight is like the breath of contented kine, stirring among the lilacs and shaking spikes of bloom, ringing the soundless bells of hyacinths dreaming briefly of Lesbos, whispering among the pale and fronded palms.

Ah, God, ah, God. The moon is a silver sickle about to mow the rose of evening from the western sky; the moon is a little silver boat on green and shoreless seas. Ave, Maria, dream. . . . How like birds with golden wings the measured bell notes fly outward and upward, passing with clear and faint regret the ultimate slender rush of cross and spire; and how like the plummet lark the echo, singing, falls. Ave, Maria. . . . Ah God, ah God, that night should come so soon.

Orion through the starry meadows strays, the creaking Wain breaks darkly through the Milky Way's faint dewed grass. Sorrow, and love that passeth away. Ave, Maria! a little silver virgin, hurt and sad and pitiful, remembering Jesus' mouth upon her breast. Mortification, and the flesh like a babe crying among dark trees . . . "hold my hair fast, and kiss me through it—so: Ah, God, ah God, ah God, that day should be soon!"

Ava, Maria; deam gratiam . . . tower of ivory, rose of Lebanon . . .

FRANKIE AND JOHNNY

Listen, Baby, before I seen you it was like I was one of them ferry boats yonder crossing and crossing a dark river or something by myself; acrossing and acrossing and never getting nowheres and not knowing it and thinking I was all the time. You know—being full of lot of names of people and things with their own business, and thinking I was the berries all the time. And say, listen:

When I seen you coming down the street back yonder it was like them two ferry boats hadn't seen each other until then, and they would stop when they met instead of crossing each other, and they would turn and go off side by side together where they wasn't nobody except them. Listen, baby; before I seen you I was just a young tough like what old Ryan, the cop, says I was, not doing nothing and not worth nothing and not caring for nothing except old Johnny. But when that drunk bum stopped you and said what he said to you and I walked up and slammed him, I done it for you and not for me; and it was like a wind had blew a lot a trash and stuff out of the street.

And when I put my arm around you and you was holding to me and crying, I knowed you was meant for me even if I hadn't never seen you before, and that I wasn't no longer the young tough like what old Ryan, the cop, says I was; and when you kissed me it was like one morning a gang of us was beating our way back to town on a rattler and the bulls jumped us and turn us off and we walked in and I seen day breaking acrost the water when it was kind of blue and dark at the same time, and the boats was still on the water

127

and there was black trees acrost, and the sky was kind of yellow and gold and blue. And a wind come over the water, making funny little sucking noises. It was like when you are in a dark room or something, and all on a sudden somebody turns up the light, and that's all. When I seen your yellow hair and your gray eyes it was like that. It was like a wind had blew clean through me and there was birds singing somewheres. And then I knowed it was all up with me.

Oh, Johnny!

Baby!

THE COBBLER

My life is a house: The smell of leather is the wall of my house. Three sides are dark, but from the other side there comes faint light through dingy unwashed windows. Beyond these windows the world grows loud and passes away. I was once a part of the world, I was once a part of the rushing river of mankind; but now I am old, I have been swirled into a still backwater in a foreign land, and the river has left me behind. That river of which I was once a part. I do not remember very well, for I am old: I have forgotten much. Joy and sorrow—what mean these? Did I know once? But joy and sorrow are the birds which whirl screaming above the rushing flood: they do not bother about backwaters. Peace I know in setting properly a nail, in fixing cunningly a sole, and in my wife. My wife? This bush of golden roses is my wife. See, how the ancient branches are twisted and gnarled with age, as this hand is twisted and gnarled and old. Yet each year it bears me sweet bloom, though it be as old in years as I.

Ah, Tuscany! and the belled flocks among the sunny hills long after the valley itself was in shadow! and feast days and dancing on the green, and she in her scarlet kerchief, her cloudy tossing hair and her sweet wild breasts arbored amid her hair! But we were promised, you see.

She and this rose and I were young together, she and I, who were promised, and a flung rose in the dust, under the evening star. But now that rose is old in a pot, and I am old and walled about with the smell of leather, and she . . . and she. . . . I have known joy and sorrows, but now I do not remember. I am old: I have forgotten much.

MAGDALEN

God, the light in my eyes, the sunlight flashing through the window, crashing in my poor head like last night's piano. Why didn't I close them damn shutters ?

I can remember when I found days gold, but now the gold of day hurts my head. 'Tis night only is gold now, and that not often. Men aint what they used to be, or money aint, or something. Or maybe its I that aint like I was once. God knows, I try to treat 'em like thay'd want I should. I treat 'em white as any, and whiter than some . . . not calling no names. I'm an American girl with an American smile I am, and they know it.

There was wild blood in my veins; when I was young the blood sang like shrill horns through me. I saw women who had the bright things I wanted . . . dresses and shoes and golden rings, lifting no finger to get them. And lights and sultry music, and all the bright chimaerae of the brain! And ah! my body like music, my body like flame crying for silken sheens a million worms had died to make, and that my body has died a hundred times to wear them. Yes, a thousand worms made this silk, and died; I have died a thousand deaths to wear it; and sometime a thousand worms, feeding upon this body which has betrayed me, feeding, will live.

Was there love once? I have forgotten her. Was there grief once? Yes, long ago. Ah, long ago.

John Gould Fletcher (1886–1950)

THE DEATH OF ENGLAND

Slowly, athwart the terrible fierce sunlight that marks a blasted summer, the body of England, rigid and stiffened in death, is borne to its last long rest.

Horse-chestnuts lift ten thousand waxen candles before it; thrushes intone their office in plaintive cadences; the faint grey-purple incense of lilac is wafted into the air; bees cease their murmurings; and the swallow, the blithe crossbearer of the sky, is silent.

From a million starving faces, pale and stunned with excess of suffering, a lonely silent plaint of irremediable misery climbs softly, like the great wailing notes of an endless De Profundis, into the ashen-blue vault of the sky.

Slowly athwart the terrible days that crawl forward to where the sun is offered up on the altar of midsummer, the body of England, broken with weariness, is borne to the slow wailings of the chant which the winds weave about it, and the dropping of wax-white petals from innumerable hawthorn trees.

Eternal rest grant her, O Lord, and the peace of the night that passes all understanding.

THE SECRET OF MARS

Some people say that the planet Mars is uninhabited. But this is not true, for I have been there and seen it.

Many centuries ago, the Martians fought their last great war; many centuries ago they organized a life scientifically perfect.

But for all that, they were not content; and their planet, like their hearts, began growing colder every year.

Then one day they suddenly decided to build a great tower to a forgotten God; and because they were weary of their machines, they decided that no stone of it should be cut by anything else but hammer and chisel and human hands.

Centuries they must have labored, for the building as it stands is immense in desolation. It is surrounded with a forest of columns for ten miles; at the intersection of enormous aisles, poised above the glory of huge leaping arches, stands the lantern-tower unfinished, ten thousand feet high.

Upon the pavement below it lies the body of the last workman, his trowel uplifted, and his hand ready to place a stone. His form is still perfect, for it is frozen in death.

On the tower rests the treasure of the perpetual snow; you would not say that Mars is uninhabited, could you hear the groans that the settling stone makes at sunrise or when the evening drifts swiftly across the barren planet.

THE WAY OF DUST

Dust, grey colorless dust, soft, fluffy, velvety, dust that sweeps over endless deserts, sweeps into the crevices of buildings, dust that emerges from beaten carpets, dust that rises from this paper, blurs my weary vision at last.

Man is the maker of dust; dust stirs beneath his feet; dust rises from the labor of his hands; dust increases in every fire he has made; dust takes all his works; the ink upon this page is only dust. In the ash-heap is salvation, and in the dust of the grave is all attainment.

Far beyond the last of the planets, beyond Orion and the Milky Way, lie shapeless clouds of dust, relics of innumerable worlds on which others have also lived and suffered. In the heart of the divine darkness this dust of the universe stirs and dances, and rekindles in itself, through perpetual movement, the germ of universal life and the light of common day.

Embracing this dust, I embrace all things; summoning forth this dust, I summon also God; desiring only this dust, I desire forever immortality.

I am but an infinitesimal particle of casual dust, and it matters nothing to my destiny if I live here amongst men or beyond the most distant star.

THE END OF JOB

After Job had been given back all his possessions, he began to grow discontented again. He had become so accustomed to arguing with God, that he now rather prided himself on his dialectical skill, and regretted that he had no one left with whom to argue, or nothing to complain about. His wife and children naturally put him down as an obstinate old fool, who did not know when he was well off, and this of course made matters worse.

To crown all, he discovered that Elihu, a perfect greenhorn who had witnessed all the contest without uttering a word, had written it up in the form of a popular novel selling in thousands, had taken good care to introduce himself as one of the speakers, and had even added some fairly effective remarks of his own.

And when Job protested that the novel was a distortion of fact, and Elihu coolly responded that he had employed an artist's license; that he had made use of certain actual incidents merely in order to illustrate a philosophy of life; and that the hero of his novel was, as a character, purely imaginary; Job became indignant.

He wandered off into the wilderness, and there started interviewing his old enemy Satan. Satan showed himself to be affable, even conciliatory, and seemed to ask only that bygones should be bygones; but he could not promise any definite help. The whirlwind, he said, had convinced him that might, if not right, was on God's side.

The next person Job applied to was his wife. "My dear, we are much too prosperous, and we really ought to get rid of some of our property," he began tactfully. But with a toss of the head she merely remarked: "Pooh, what nonsense!"

The three friends proved equally refractory. Two of them refused even to speak to him, considering him an object beneath contempt; the third who happened to be suffering from a slight shortage of funds, owing to a drought the year previously, listened carefully to what Job said, assured him that there was much in his arguments, but counseled patience. He then suggested that Job might lend him a considerable sum, which having obtained, he promptly departed. Nor did he ever again put in an appearance. So Job became more discontented than ever, and now he was neglected by all. His hair and beard grew more and more long and matted; he never cut his nails, and never washed. His countenance became more and more frequently tinged with the effects of drink, and his remarks maudlin. His seven sons and three daughters, who now managed the estate, severely restricted his pocket-money, scarcely allowing him to enter the house, and even spoke of putting him under restraint.

One day, however, Job was discovered trying to set fire to his own house, and was hauled before the police-court. His wife and children, in order to avoid a scandal, tried to persuade the judge to release him on the grounds that he was irresponsible, but before their pleas had any effect, Job's body was discovered hanging in his cell.

Charles Henri Ford (1908–2002)

SUITE

after after not at all times and ever but the next seven ante meri-
diem then when the yellow-on-green light emergingly oblique
denied the brittle air: then the underside of fingers took a slight
touch on a doorknob the wristbone tremulous there was the bed
there was the body the purple mouth the blood and saliva on the
pillow in one small circle of disgrace. as for me i held my breath
in the center of my lungs and drew consciousness back into my
brain until i felt a kernel there for this is the way i thought i cant
be crying i cant be twisting my fingers but no one will see how
deeply nails can sink into palms so, so many afters have gone before
so many afters are to be and this is what is happening: im not (in
a rear) drunk (room): in a (drunk?) slotmachine: im not drunk: i
have kissed vulgarity i am not ashamed: this is what is happening:
turn your head querulousy, look at the clock: you will not know
what time it is. we cant go ninetyfive miles an hour and care: there-
fore. he sells stuff for his papa jane wrote virginia hes been work-
ing in the garden it is wonderful how he does can you beat that
working in the and eightyeight years stop passing the tomatoes
every time i look around youre passing me the tomatoes. get nerv-
ous, dearie. cry your eyes out over the keyboard and say it's not
worth being bitter about. there was a tightness across the heart
and i felt something go snap. if it gets too bad we'll stay drunk

how many days and eat large tbonesteaks and then go to pieces. distriction won: boutiful she sad with her mith. there was a witwet on the drodress and i told her youre a bigirl noo: i set anna your a big curl nooow.   a line striverring at the ans of graysalver smick strangled desonostrils. he pit. paddered. pont. (she said she dreamed all the *time* of a large-negro-with-pink-lips chasing her.) the sun gives light : that was the sun's light on my eyelids, not your fingers; that was gin in my temples, not your arms around my head. ordinarily i would have known.   chicago is not a town to sneer at neither to grow sentimental over: you can stand under the el at five or fivethirty or six and talk as loud as you want to and nobody will hear you: at night walking on michigan avenue nobody will see you for the automobiles rush by too fast and if you take it to your room it might say itaintnatural but anyway curse a in memphis who had the and if you dont believe it i'll show you.   yes i sat beside him in the darkness with my face like white silk. daytimes i am by myself and play the victrola.   but before that i couldnt have said could i i couldnt have come right out like that and said i dont love you anymore im sorry darling but i dont.   because your mouth covers mine when we kiss. for even after that in bed i thought yes. yes i do. yes i . . do. i do. last night was different. there were shoulders that touched, not lips. that one said whats the matter did you just get us and i said no do i look sleepy. of course it wasnt sleep or lack of it that made my eyes look that way . . . i like to feel my hands on cheeks . . . screaming over longdistance *but dar-ling, why?* . . . do not ask me if i care no more for wilde and let us go down to the store and select a suit. there is so little to do here. all day yesterday i listened to ethel waters on the victrola crying am i blue forgetting a body still still and rigid with the dope in the veins not mattering.

FLAG OF ECSTASY

(for Marcel Duchamp)

Over the towers of autoerotic honey, over the dungeons of homicidal drives, over the pleasures of invading sleep, over the sorrows of invading a woman, over the voix céleste, over vomito negro, over the unendurable sensation of madness, over the insatiable sense of sin, over the spirit of uprisings, over the bodies of tragediennes, over tarantism: "melancholy stupor and an uncontrollable desire to dance," over all. . . .

Over ambivalent virginity, over unfathomable succubi, over the tormentors of Negresses, over openhearted sans-culottes, over a stactometer for the tears of France, over unmanageable hermaphrodites, over the sun's lascivious serum, over the sewers of the moon, over the saints of debauchery, over criminals made of gold, over the princes of delirium, over the paupers of peace, over signs foretelling the end of the world, over signs foretelling the beginning of a world, like one of those tender strips of flesh, on either side of the vertebral column, Marcel, wave!

MESSAGE TO RIMBAUD

Your summerhouse of underdone meat is still standing, boy. The last time I went by, a note was tacked on the door. It read: "Bleed for me!" There was no signature, but I recognized Humanity's handwriting.

Jane Heap (1883–1964)

SKETCHES

White

I

Sharp, empty air. . . . Out of the black mouths of engines white smoke rises on thin stems into white ghosts of ancient trees; together they rise into ghosts of ancient forests, sway and surge and are gone again a million years.

II

The hot air of the day stays in the city until night. The long slope of my roof presses the heat down upon me. Soon it will rain. But there is no rest in me: my heart is wandering too far. My friends may still be in the city, but I do not seek them. I go to the animals in the park. Within their enclosures black shadows of camels lie in the darkness. A great white camel broods in the moonlight, apart from the rest. His lonely eyes are closed and he moves his head slowly from side to side on his long neck, swaying in pain, searching in a dream for his lost world. I have seen a Norwegian ship carrying its carved head through the waters of a fjord with such a movement. . . .

Now the high clouds cover the moon. Out on the lake a wind assails the layers of heat. A white peacock sits in a tree, aloof, elegant, incorruptible. . . . A light green spirit. . . . Across the first thunder he lifts his long white laugh at us like a maniac.

Void

I cannot live long in your city: it has no zones of pain for me where I may rest, no places where old joys dwell and I may suffer. It is as empty for me as the honeycomb cliff cities of the Southwest. For I shall not know love again in this or any place.

PARIS AT ONE TIME

Naked and transparent negroes, taller than the tour Eiffel, play ball with apricot-colored cubes . . . against a cobalt sky.

A typhoon . . . purple-green, whirling . . . an inverted pine tree. Ah! it is a Christmas tree with all our gifts upon it. It sways and is sucked into the sea—disappears.

The earth slants up in a plane to the farthest place in the sky. Open mummy-cases in exact rows . . . all the queens of the world, their heads turned to the left . . . lie listening forever to our words of love . . . a smile of unbelief upon their painted profiles.

The wind gently lifts them from their caskets . . . they become tall plume-pens of many colours . . . emerald, blue, yellow, black, cerise. They write in the sand, something that has been forgotten. No one moves them but they continue to write and slowly the Champs Elysées appears in the foreground . . . Rousseau-like people go walking up and down. A long line of carrousels slowly fades into place, down the centre of the avenue . . . from the Arch to the Concorde. They are painted and golden, but silent and curtained and motionless. All at once all of the people, walking on the paths and in the groves, begin to move slowly towards the carrousels . . . when everyone has disappeared inside the curtains, a silent music begins to play. The curtains are lifted for a moment . . . there are no horses, no pigs, or chariots. There are two great spiral blades: giant augers. The people stand stupidly upon them and wait. The spirals begin to revolve. They dig themselves rapidly down into the earth. . . everything disappears. The music too is under the ground.

A pack of red rabbits comes bounding out of a grove at the right. Their ears back. Their bodies a straight line of speed. They are stopped in the air. They strain to another leap. They are compelled to remain motionless. A smile of indifference points their faces. They slowly change to glistening fish. They fall into a long line . . . abreast. They close their eyes and swim towards the river, singing softly in the night.

Ernest Hemingway (1899–1961)

from IN OUR TIME

Chapter I

Everybody was drunk. The whole battery was drunk going along the road in the dark. We were going to the Champagne. The lieutenant kept riding his horse out into the fields and saying to him, "I'm drunk, I tell you, mon vieux. Oh, I am so soused." We went along the road all night in the dark and the adjutant kept riding up alongside my kitchen and saying, "You must put it out. It is dangerous. It will be observed." We were fifty kilometers from the front but the adjutant worried about the fire in my kitchen. It was funny going along that road. That was when I was a kitchen corporal.

Chapter II

Minarets stuck up in the rain out of Adrianople across the mud flats. The carts were jammed for thirty miles along the Karagatch road. Water buffalo and cattle were hauling carts through the mud. No end and no beginning. Just carts loaded with everything they owned. The old men and women, soaked through, walked along keeping the cattle moving. The Maritza was running yellow almost up to the bridge. Carts were jammed solid on the bridge with camels bobbing along through them. Greek cavalry herded along the procession. Women and kids were in the carts crouched with mattresses, mirrors, sewing machines, bundles. There was a woman having a kid with a young girl holding a blanket over her and crying. Scared sick looking at it. It rained all through the evacuation.

Chapter III

We were in a garden at Mons. Young Buckley came in with his patrol from across the river. The first German I saw climbed up over the garden wall. We waited till he got one leg over and then potted him. He had so much equipment on and looked awfully surprised and fell down into the garden. Then three more came over further down the wall. We shot them. They all came just like that.

Chapter IV

It was a frightfully hot day. We'd jammed an absolutely perfect barricade across the bridge. It was simply priceless. A big old wrought-iron grating from the front of a house. Too heavy to lift and you could shoot through it and they would have to climb over it. It was absolutely topping. They tried to get over it, and we potted them from forty yards. They rushed it, and officers came out alone and worked on it. It was an absolutely perfect obstacle. Their officers were very fine. We were frightfully put out when we heard the flank had gone, and we had to fall back.

Chapter V

They shot the six cabinet ministers at half-past six in the morning against the wall of a hospital. There were pools of water in the courtyard. There were wet dead leaves on the paving of the courtyard. It rained hard. All the shutters of the hospital were nailed shut. One of the ministers was sick with typhoid. Two soldiers carried him downstairs and out into the rain. They tried to hold him up against the wall but he sat down in a puddle of water. The other five stood very quietly against the wall. Finally the officer told the soldiers it was no good trying to make him stand up. When they fired the first volley he was sitting down in the water with his head on his knees.

L'Envoi

The king was working in the garden. He seemed very glad to see me. We walked through the garden. This is the queen, he said. She was clipping a rose bush. Oh how do you do, she said. We sat down at a table under a big tree and the king ordered whiskey and soda. We have good whiskey anyway, he said. The revolutionary committee, he told me, would not allow him to go outside the palace grounds. Plastiras is a very good man I believe, he said, but frightfully difficult. I think he did right though shooting those chaps. If Kerensky had shot a few men things might have been altogether different. Of course the great thing in this sort of an affair is not to be shot oneself!

It was very jolly. We talked for a long time. Like all Greeks he wanted to go to America.

Fenton Johnson (1888–1958)

AFRICAN NIGHTS

TIRED

I am tired of work; I am tired of building up somebody else's civilization.

Let us take a rest, M'Lissy Jane.

I will go down to the Last Chance Saloon, drink a gallon or two of gin, shoot a game or two of dice and sleep the rest of the night on one of Mike's barrels.

You will let the old shanty go to rot, the white people's clothes turn to dust, and the Calvary Baptist Church sink to the bottomless pit.

You will spend your days forgetting you married me and your nights hunting the warm gin Mike serves the ladies in the rear of the Last Chance Saloon.

Throw the children into the river; civilization has given us too many. It is better to die than it is to grow up and find out that you are colored.

Pluck the stars out of the heavens. The stars mark our destiny. The stars marked my destiny.

I am tired of civilization.

AUNT HANNAH JACKSON

Despite her sixty years Aunt Hannah Jackson rubs on other people's clothes.

Time has played havoc with her eyes and turned to gray her parched hair.

But her tongue is nimble as she talks to herself.

All day she talks to herself about her neighbors and her friends and the man she loved.

Yes, Aunt Hannah Jackson loved even as you and I and Wun Hop Sing.

"He was a good man," she says, "but a fool."

"So am I a fool and Mrs. Lee a fool and this Mrs. Goldstein that I work for a fool."

"All of us are fools."

For rubbing on other people's clothes Aunt Hannah Jackson gets a dollar and fifty cents a day and a worn out dress on Christmas.

For talking to herself Aunt Hannah Jackson gets a smile as we call her a good natured fool.

Aunt Jane Allen

State Street is lonely today. Aunt Jane Allen has driven her chariot to Heaven.

I remember how she hobbled along, a little woman, parched of skin, brown as the leather of a satchel and with eyes that had scanned eighty years of life.

Have those who bore her dust to the last resting place buried with her the basket of aprons she went up and down State Street trying to sell?

Have those who bore her dust to the last resting place buried with her the gentle word Son that she gave to each of the seed of Ethiopia?

The Barber

I wield the razor, sling hot towels and talk.

My daily newspaper is the racing chart and my pastime making bets on fleet-footed horses.

Whatever is left from betting I divide with my wife and a yellow woman who lives in an apartment on Wabash Avenue.

(Poor Wife! She gets very little.)

I love gay clothes, a good supply of Fatimas and the fire in gin and whiskey.

I love life. Who doesn't?

The Drunkard

I had a wife, but she is gone. She left me a week ago. God bless her!

I married another in the rear of Mike's saloon. It was a gallon jug of the reddest liquor that ever burned the throat of man. I will be true to my new wife. You can have the other.

The Banjo Player

There is music in me, the music of a peasant people.

I wander through the levee, picking my banjo and singing my songs of the cabin and the field. At the Last Chance Saloon I am as welcome as the violets in March; there is always food and drink for me there, and the dimes of those who love honest music. Behind the railroad tracks the little children clap their hands and love me as they love Kris Kringle.

But I fear that I am a failure. Last night a woman called me a troubadour. What is a troubadour?

The Minister

I mastered pastoral theology, the Greek of the Apostles, and all the difficult subjects in a minister's curriculum.

I was as learned as any in this country when the Bishop ordained me.

And I went to preside over Mount Moriah, largest flock in the Conference.

I preached the Word as I felt it, I visited the sick and dying and comforted the afflicted in spirit.

I loved my work because I loved my God.

But I lost my charge to Sam Jenkins, who has not been to school four years in his life.

I lost my charge because I could not make my congregation shout.

And my dollar money was small, very small.

Sam Jenkins can tear a Bible to tatters and his congregation destroys the pews with their shouting and stamping.

Sam Jenkins leads in the gift of raising dollar money.

Such is religion.

Once I was good like the Virgin Mary and the Minister's wife.

My father worked for Mr. Pullman and white people's tips ; but he died two days after his insurance expired.

I had nothing, so I had to go to work.

All the stock I had was a white girl's education and a face that enchanted the men of both races.

Starvation danced with me.

So when Big Lizzie, who kept a house for white men, came to me with tales of fortune that I could reap from the sale of my virtue I bowed my head to Vice.

Now I can drink more gin than any man for miles around.

Gin is better than all the water in Lethe.

Amy Lowell (1874–1925)

BATH

The day is fresh-washed and fair, and there is a smell of tulips and narcissus in the air.

The sunshine pours in at the bath-room window and bores through the water in the bathtub in lathes and planes of greenish-white. It cleaves the water into flaws like a jewel, and cracks it to bright light.

Little spots of sunshine lie on the surface of the water and dance, dance, and their reflections wobble deliciously over the ceiling; a stir of my finger sets them whirring, reeling. I move a foot, and the planes of light in the water jar. I lie back and laugh, and let the green-white water, the sun-flawed beryl water, flow over me. The day is almost too bright to bear, the green water covers me from the too bright day. I will lie here awhile and play with the water and the sun spots.

The sky is blue and high. A crow flaps by the window, and there is a whiff of tulips and narcissus in the air.

BREAKFAST TABLE

In the fresh-washed sunlight, the breakfast table is decked and white. It offers itself in flat surrender, tendering tastes, and smells, and colors, and metals, and grains, and the white cloth falls over its side, draped and wide. Wheels of white glitter in the silver coffee-pot, hot and spinning like catherine-wheels, they whirl, and twirl—and my eyes begin to smart, the little white, dazzling wheels prick them like darts. Placid and peaceful, the rolls of bread spread themselves in the sun to bask. A stack of butter-pats, pyramidal, shout orange through the white, scream, flutter, call: "Yellow! Yellow! Yellow!" Coffee steam rises in a stream, clouds the silver tea-service with mist, and twists up into the sunlight, revolved, involuted, suspiring higher and higher, fluting in a thin spiral up the high blue sky. A crow flies by and croaks at the coffee steam. The day is new and fair with good smells in the air.

WALK

Over the street the white clouds meet, and sheer away without touching.

On the sidewalks, boys are playing marbles. Glass marbles, with amber and blue hearts, roll together and part with a sweet clashing noise. The boys strike them with black and red striped agates. The glass marbles spit crimson when they are hit, and slip into the gutters under rushing brown water. I smell tulips and narcissus in the air, but there are no flowers anywhere, only white dust whipping up the street, and a girl with a gay Spring hat and blowing skirts. The dust and the wind flirt at her ankles and her neat, high-heeled patent leather shoes. Tap, tap, the little heels pat the pavement, and the wind rustles among the flowers on her hat.

A water-cart crawls slowly on the other side of the way. It is green and gay with new paint, and rumbles contentedly, sprinkling clear water over the white dust. Clear zigzagging water, which smells of tulips and narcissus.

The thickening branches make a pink *grisaille* against the blue sky.

Whoop! The clouds go dashing at each other and sheer away just in time. Whoop! And a man's hat careers down the street in front of the white dust, leaps into the branches of a tree, veers away and trundles ahead of the wind, jarring the sunlight into spokes of rose-color and green.

A motor-car cuts a swathe through the bright air, sharp-beaked, irresistible, shouting to the wind to make way. A glare of dust and sunshine tosses together behind it, and settles down. The sky is quiet and high, and the morning is fair with fresh-washed air.

MIDDAY AND AFTERNOON

Swirl of crowded streets. Shock and recoil of traffic. The stock-still brick facade of an old church, against which the waves of people lurch and withdraw. Flare of sunshine down side-streets. Eddies of light in the windows of chemists' shops, with their blue, gold, purple jars, darting colors far into the crowd. Loud bangs and tremors, murmurings out of high windows, whirring of machine belts, blurring of horses and motors. A quick spin and shudder of brakes on an electric car, and the jar of a churchbell knocking against the metal blue of the sky. I am a piece of the town, a bit of blown dust, thrust along with the crowd. Proud to feel the pavement under me, reeling with feet. Feet tripping, skipping, lagging, dragging, plodding doggedly, or springing up and advancing on firm elastic insteps. A boy is selling papers, I smell them clean and new from the press. They are fresh like the air, and pungent as tulips and narcissus.

The blue sky pales to lemon, and great tongues of gold blind the shop-windows, putting out their contents in a flood of flame.

Robert McAlmon (1896–1956)

VILLAGE

The saloons are all closed now. Boards are across their doorways. Spiderwebs hang across the broken panes of glass.

Al Wilson would not have cared though if he were alive today. Long before prohibition was ever considered his wife had him blacklisted at all the saloons, and told the grocers not to sell him extracts of any sort; not to sell him anything in fact. She forced him to the cornsilos.

Poor gentile Mrs. Wilson! She had no cornsilo to make her forget her straits. She was a desolate figure, not made for desolation either. To the last she would wear gloves, neatly patched; would go to church every Sunday and march with dignity up the aisle to sing with her quavery soprano in the choir. To the last she would make calls and ask ladies to call upon her. She at least could do the correct thing if Alfred was a town character.

Other men—the tobacco chewers spitting from their benches at the livery stable, the church Deacon Davis whose walk home was ceremonial with hat lifting and circumspect gallantry, and with talks about the new minister, for there was never a time when there was not a new minister—the other men, drinkers too but not "addicts," would, between their pool games, and talk about getting a new postoffice for the town, reminisce about the time when the Wilsons were first married. Everybody was so sure Alfred would make congress—so fine a gentleman, and so brilliant a young attorney, "promising, Ha, Ha, Ha, but promises ain't allus kept," Gus the horseshoer would blow out over his tongue of snuff. Poor Al! no gitting around the fact that Mrs. Wilson was a charming woman, soft voice and so accomplished a musician—too nice; the ruination of Al!

Now all the Wilsons had was five children, and one of them not quite right. Alfred drunk, it was said, when—O yes, a sad case, a sad case.

The saloons are closed now. Last summer one young attorney shot himself because life was so dull in the old town, and a living so hard to make. "He didn't have likker to cheer him up like Al Wilson did in his young days," Gus told me, as always, over his cud of Copenhagen snuff.

There may be other restless ones. One boy used to tell me that I was the only one "to understand." Understand? I could see that he was becoming one more of the restless ones—to what end?—but what is the end of an end?

Cobwebs and dusty broken window panes are in so many deserted buildings in the old town. Even the mudhole in which I learned to swim is dry, life is so dry, dust dry there.

FIRE BUG

Ho, you Christmas Tree burning in the street, casting the light of your flames upon the carcass of that horse which died of the cold or of old age—or just died perhaps because he wanted to—you are burning clear and clean. How does it happen? Green needles snap to bright orange flames—pale bright orange—or is it blue, or purple, who knows what the color of a flame is—or of a flame's aura—and of all auras of its heat's irradiations that force the cold out and away from all sides of it.

Fir tree on fire, I wish your conflagration would spread, catch the buildings around you, leap to the church spires, run along the telephone wires to the skyscrapers—burn, burn, burn, keep burning clean and clear and let me stand. Your bright flames burning all civilization to clean ashes. All moralities, and all non-moralities; all traditions and all rebellions. I want to be clear with emptiness—to be bending over where the fire has been, burning my hands in clean ashes that blow away in the cold air when I lift my palms opened upward to the sky. Ashes—beautiful ashes—and around me, nothing, nothing, nothing—and the wind will sweep even the sky away. Then there will be only I with my wishes, and they will be the reality and the only reality, and I will be cleansed.

O there is nobody else I care about, fir tree on fire. Burn and with your clear fire, bring me that desire for a Christmas present and whenever—it will not be belated.

THE ARTIFICIAL LAKE

Across the corrugated surface of the waters actually calm beneath their slight ripple toy steamers chug, in straight lines. The arrogantly coy swans stir with unwilling dignity from their paths, eyeing the intruders with a curiosity not so cute as that of the plump caressable ducks, one of which has had to cease pointing its pintail at the sky and swim in frenzy out of a streamer's way.

This is a day of plump and comfortable contentments.

PLOUGHED LAND

The clean barrenness of soils affects me strangely, as I stand looking across a thousand acres of new-turned soil.

One could stand in the middle of that raw earth, in the middle of the earth—and the centre of the earth must be where one is—and shout, breathe exuberantly, yodel, sing—and who shall say that it is not great singing—curse—maybe one would not be permanently happy, or free—but there would be clear air to breathe, and noise to make.

Even if they are alive and of today there is something archeological about the plough, plough horses and their driver standing an eighth of a mile away. Let them move and toil, but do not speak to them. They are well enough as a design for some fountain but as for intimacy——

No, no, breathe the sky—let the sun play over-passionately with your body——.

Whoops, mah boy, the sacrosanct portals of that liberty and situation where the bricklayer is sacristan to civilization, with the butcher and tailor high up in command; and the moon pishes and piddles down upon liberated lovers debating the number of offspring advisable in their economic position! We're out of the rut of rusticity plotting with masons and diplomats of the coal shovel how to settle all our affairs more comfortably.

Lots of rain. That's what the farmers want. They are pleased, let it be remarked, with what the sheep come to out on the meadows. Many new lambs. Much greater profit this year. That is evident.

She's a woman with lots of push I've heard. The kind to make a good wife. A woman with lots of push is what a man should have now that prices are so high. Etc., etc., etc.

Answering yours of the nth instant. No! Yours very truly. Good—ye.

HISTORY PROFESSOR

"Now in the interests of scholarships—uh huh—yes—in the interests of scholarship" he'd lecture, asking for bibliography, collateral reading, and annotations, which requests never interfered with students' thoughts on Saturday night dances, or Monday night drunk-ons.

It's a shame, kiddo, I'll tell you it's a shame that jazzy people like Alexander, Cleopatra, Hannibal, and Henry the Eighth should be annotated thus by a male pedagogue who wears his winter underwear through June, and uses a Pinkham pill for a laxative twice a week to keep his system in order.

Kenneth Patchen (1911–1972)

POLLY—AN ALMOST-TRUE STORY

Polly had a kind of electric beauty—it flashed out of her eye and ran up and down over her face like little mice coated with jewels.

Polly was in love with a teamster who used to ride around in front of her house on Sunday in a red buckboard pulled by two blood-ed mares. He never looked in but he would whistle "Painted lips, painted eyes, she's just a bird of paradise" and then whip the mares into a fireman's waggle.

For some reason this made Polly very angry. She would walk back into the parlor and grab her little brother away from the funny papers and clamp him into a tub of cold water. This always sur-prised her mother, so Polly got into the habit of having two tubs ready. Sometimes the old man would be home, and that'd make three tubs. Anyone happen in—they'd get a tub. It went on like that until one Sunday the red buckboard didn't show up. Polly's folks were much relieved, of course; and Polly was just as pretty as ever. Three weeks later they found the teamster in a little dump of elderberry bushes near the road. Someone had taken a knife and damn near sliced off his head. What happened to the buckboard and the two mares is just another one of those things that nobody ever seems able to get to the bottom of.

FAMILY PORTRAIT

Great tarry wings splatter grayly up out of the blinding glare of the open-hearth furnaces. In the millyard the statue of some old bastard with a craggy grin is turning shit-colored above the bowed heads of the night shift that comes crunching in between the piles of slag. That's my father washing at the kitchen sink. The grimy water runs into the matted hair of his belly. The smell of scorched cloth and sweat adds its seasoning to the ham and cabbage. The muscles of his back ripple like great ropes of greased steel. An awesome thing to see! Yet he never raised his hand in anger against any man—which was a very lucky thing. A soapy snort escapes him with the sound of a thunderclap, and my kid sister vigorously rattles the lid of a pot. In the parlor my grandfather lies, two days dead. "Aye, and the only statue for him's a spade in 'is stumpy teeth now."—"A lapful of withered nuts to make the muckin' grasses grow . . ."—"Hush you are, for here be the priest with his collar so tidy and lady-clean."—Liked his bit of drink, Hughey did, God take the long thirst out of his soul and all."

I myself remember once after a brush with Mrs. Hannan, who happened to be passing hard under his window one morning, he told me, "Ah, there's only one thing worse than the rich, my lad . . . and that's the poor, and that's the ruckin', lyin', unmannerin', snivelin' poor, my lad!" and a great whip of tobacco juice lashed out onto the tar-topped road.

On, on into the small hours went the singing and the laughing and the gay, wonderful story-telling . . . and all the while the candle wax dripped slowly down on my grandfather's shiny black Sunday suit.

O WHAT A REVOLUTION!

It is remarkable but it is no less painful for that, how rarely people make an effort not to understand "things." They start well.

Children say "Why doesn't grandpa grow no beard like a cow huh?" and they're told "Because he doesn't have to, that's why." or "Why is grass always the color of engine oil and conjugations of cigarette?"—"Because your papa's a sloppy, ill-tempered bastard and I'd shoot him in a minute if my particular brand of sex had any appeal for the insurance man."

Children don't want "to know," they want to increase their enjoyment of not knowing. But people will go on Thursdaying on Wednesdays.

What precisely is "a tree"? What *does* the grass "mean"? Why are snowflakes snowflakes? Why do animals have *"faces"*?

These are not casual questions. Think about them. Then tell me what conclusion you reach. To the first person sending in a satisfactory answer to any or all of these questions, I will pay the sum of one million dollars. So think them over, won't you?

THERE ARE TWO

Ways about it. In fact, that only scratches the surface; for—well, had you seen the weeds, the weeds—even those weeds growing just below the outer edge of the wall! that would fix you! Crested . . . tubular . . . a few with—well, sort of hands . . .

In fact, I told my friend Flip, "Flip, you've got to do something about those weeds, especially those weeds down there just under the stains along the wall by the gate." But as usual he was monkeying around the car. It was almost dark by the time he got downstairs again, and the first thing he said was: "Do you want that other set of pipes inside, or do you want them curled around the hood?"

I told him curled around would be just dandy as a pair of little pink panties.

So. You know how it is. Sure, I had come there looking for that elusive oyster, happiness. Yep, that's what I was after, that goddam little sad-faced, buck-toothed oyster, happiness. And what had I got? Do I *really* have to tell you?

After a while I went out and climbed up on the wall. It had started to rain again. Pretty soon it was coming down in the large economy size buckets. I tore up all my identification papers and stripped down to where I had only one shoe and my hat on. Then

I stood up on my hind legs and shouted: "So! Enough's enough, you lousy, scrounging bastards! I'm off to join the Indians, see!" Then taking my other shoe off, I added: "And while you're at it, to hell with the Indians too!"

WHEN WE WERE HERE TOGETHER

When we were here together in a place we did not know, nor one another.

A bit of grass held between the teeth for a moment, bright hair on the wind. What we were we did not know, nor ever the grass or the flame of hair turning to ash on the wind.

But they lied about that. From the beginning they lied. To the child, telling him that there was somewhere anger against him, and a hatred against him, and only for the reason of his being in the world. But never did they tell him that the only evil and danger was in themselves; that they alone were the poisoners and the betrayers; that they—they *alone*—were responsible for what was being done in the world.

And they told the child to starve and to kill the child that was within him; for only by doing this could he safely enter their world; only by doing this could he become a useful and adjusted member of the community which they had prepared for him. And this time, alas, they did not lie.

And with the death of the child was born a thing that had neither the character of a man nor the character of a child, but was a horrible and monstrous parody of the two; and it is in his world now that the flesh of man's spirit lies twisted and despoiled under the indifferent stars.

When we were here together in a place we did not know, nor one another. O green this bit of warm grass between our teeth—O beautiful the hair of our mortal goddess on the indifferent wind.

A PASTURIZED SCENE

A little roly poly Giant Sloth chanced to be picking a bouquet of dryish blue skullcaps, when, without any warning whatever, an impetuous Cow dashed from a doorway hung with swinging bags and began at once to make wild threats against his continued safety. Much enamored as he was by their vague, barny smell and puffy sponge-veined lips, he made in turn a most charming but nonethemore sincere gesture of offering the blossoms to her sharply divided attention. But the chuffling moocomer, who knew a sport, however natural, when she saw one, immediately thrust the poor little Giant Sloth into a nest handed her by old Bluff Durham, her everattentive husband, and went heelsbelling off to the market. For, you see, only the day before, while botheredly fly-ing past a shopwindow, she had noticed a pair of magnificent, shocking-pink panties, which she had every reason to believe would make her the season's most spectacular social bust.

Laura Riding (1901–1991)

WILLIAM AND DAISY:
FRAGMENT OF A FINISHED NOVEL

William and Daisy lived in Cemetery Street. They had no con-
nection with each other except that they were not attracted by life
or death; so they lived in Cemetery Street. William was pessimistic
because he disliked life a little more than death, Daisy was opti-
mistic because she disliked death a little more than life. William
had two memories: one, that he had been familiar with harlots; two,
that he had been familiar with famous writers. These two memo-
ries mixed and he could make nothing of them. Daisy had two
memories: one, that she had once been a harlot; two, that she had
in her time known several famous writers. These two memories
mixed and she could make nothing of them. They could make
nothing of their memories except that they both felt dignified and
did not wish to end their days in a workhouse. So they lived in
Cemetery Street.

Every night Daisy went for a walk down Cemetery Street and
said "What a lovely night," and passed William on her walk and
said "What a coincidence"; and every night William, too, said
"What a lovely night" and "What a coincidence." They began to
know each other's thoughts and were more bored with each other
than ever.

They had their shoes mended by the same shoemaker. Each

knew the shoemaker had taken a girl to live with him behind the shop and then thrown her into the street when his wife had learned about it. Yet each continued to think him a nice man because they could not be bothered to think him a mean man. They became more and more absolute in their thoughts and habits until . . .

I do not know what happened to them, nor do they.

HUNGRY TO HEAR

Hungry to hear (like Jew-faces, kind but anticipating pain) they sit, their ears raw. The conversation remains genteel, of motor cars: her brother bought a car, he was having a six months' vacation from an Indian post, he should have known better than to buy an American car, the value depreciates so, and *she* (his sister) should not have lent it to *her* (her friend) even though it wasn't her fault that the car only did fifteen miles to the gallon after she returned it. A clear situation like this, in which life is easy to understand, is cruel to them. It leaves no scratches in the mind around which opinions, sympathies, silly repetitions can fester and breed dreams and other remote infections—too remote always to give serious pain. They long to be fumbled, to have confusion and uncertainty make a confused and uncertain end of them. There they sit, having pins-and-needles of obscurity which they mistake for sensation. They open their newspapers: "I suppose it is foolish to spend all this time reading newspapers? They are lying and dishonest and devoted to keeping a certain portion of the population in ignorance and intellectual slavery? Or is it foolish to take it so seriously? I shall go on reading them out of sophistication? . . ." Oh, go to hell.

IN A CAFÉ

This is the second time I have seen that girl here. What makes me suspicious is that her manner has not changed. From her ears I should say she is Polish. If this is so, is it not dangerous to drink coffee here? Does anyone else think of this, I wonder? Yet why should I be suspicious? And why should her manner not remain unchanged? She has probably been cold, unhappy, unsuccessful or simply not alive ever since I saw her last. Quite honestly I wish her success. The man who is making sketches from pictures in the Art Magazine may find her little Polish ears not repulsive. For good luck I turn away and do not look at her again. I, who am neither sluttish nor genteel, like this place because it has brown curtains of a shade I do not like. Everything, even my position, which is not against the wall, is unsatisfactory and pleasing: the men coming too hurriedly, the women too comfortably from the lavatories, which are in an unnecessarily prominent position—all this is disgusting; it puts me in a sordid good-humor. This attitude I find to be the only way in which I can defy my own intelligence. Otherwise I should become barbaric and be a modern artist and intelligently mind everything, or I should become civilized and be a Christian Scientist and intelligently mind nothing. Plainly the only problem is to avoid that love of lost identity which drives so many clever people to hold difficult points of view—by *difficult* I mean big, hungry, religious points of view which absorb their personality. I for one am resolved to mind or not mind only to the degree where my point of view is no larger than myself. I can thus have a great number of points of view, like fingers, and which I can treat as I treat the fingers of my hand, to hold my cup, to tap the table for me and fold themselves away when I do not wish to think. If I fold them away now, then I am sitting here all this time (without ordering a second cup) because other people go on sitting here, not because I am thinking. It is all indeed, I admit, rather horrible. But if I remain a person instead of becoming a point of view, I have no contact with horror. If I become a point of view, I become a force and am brought into direct contact with horror, another force. As well set one plague of cats loose upon another and expect peace of it. As a force I have power, as a person virtue. All forces eventually commit suicide with their power, while virtue in a person merely gives him a small though constant pain from being continuously touched, looked at, mentally handled; a pain by which he learns to recognize himself. Poems, being more like persons, probably only squirm every time they are read and wrap themselves round more tightly. Pictures and pieces of music, being more like forces, are soon worn out by the power that holds them together. To me pictures and music are always like stories told backwards: or like this I read in the newspaper: "Up to the last she retained all her faculties and was able to sign cheques."

It is surely time for me to go and yet I do not in the least feel like going. I have been through certain intimacies and small talk with everything here, when I go out I shall have to begin all over again in the street, in addition to wondering how many people are being run over behind me; when I get home I shall turn on the light and say to myself how glad I am it is winter, with no moths to kill. And I shall look behind the curtain where my clothes hang and think that I have done this ever since the homicidal red-haired boy confided his fear to me and I was sorry for him and went to his room and did it for him. And my first look round will be a Wuthering-Heights look; after that I shall settle down to work and forget about myself.

I am well aware that we form, all together, one monster. But I refuse to giggle and I refuse to be frightened and I refuse to be fierce. Nor will I feed or be fed on. I will simply think of other things. I will go now. Let them stare. I am well though eccentrically dressed.

Edouard Roditi (1910–1992)

METAMORPHOSIS

There were no more faces.

One day above the western gate of the city there appeared a grey cloud shaped like a hand. As the hand came nearer it was seen to hold a glove; and when the hand was above the city like a dark sun at its noon, the glove fell.

Immediately all faces disappeared. A man who was buying an umbrella first became aware of this; he raised his head and saw that the salesman's face had been replaced by a large oval green leaf. He looked at his own face in a mirror and saw that it had also been replaced by a large oval green leaf.

The alarm was given. Men ceased to disagree over this or that. The goldfish in the bowl in Mrs. X's drawing-room ceased to think that they were the centre of the universe. All machines stopped and several dogs and cats were seen to fall down dead in the streets. Then the clock on the cathedral tower began to turn backwards. Stocks fell on the market and there was a general panic when people noticed that all the tickers and the radios were silent.

Ever since that day we have all been vegetarians; but it is forbidden by law to eat the large oval green bay-leaf.

SÉANCE

The stranger walks into the dark room where two men sit at the table and talk of travel. The stranger joins in the conversation saying: "I too have traveled"; and the two men look up and seem surprised at his sudden appearance. In the corner of the ceiling there is a sound of very swift wings, or of a muttering of motors and a chattering of thin voices. The stranger disappears. His voice is heard first in this corner, then in that, until it finally fades away somewhere near the small open window. Where the stranger stood the two men find a railway-ticket to an unknown destination.

OLD WIVES' TALE

The network of twigs is etched against the background of the dying day. In the dark undergrowth, the invisible beasts of the night are stirring the leaves and a warm moist breath attacks the hand with sudden fear of hidden teeth.

On the cold road, the rising moon shouts: "Ice". Not so long ago, the moon was red, or rather the damp summer had called forth an eczema of rust on the moon's pale steel face. But tonight the pale moon shouts "Ice" on the ice-white road which sleeps and dreams of legless and bodiless feet that run at random and forget their birth by pairs.

Feet and eyes and ears and legs and hands and arms are born by pairs. But the night tolerates the birth of single limbs and organs and its bushes are full of one-eyed beasts—have they a head, a body?—; then there are lonely ears listening in the flowers, and one eye watches you sometimes from between their petals.

Do not touch flowers at night. Do not speak to flowers at night. Do not walk abroad at night; but sleep and forget the dangers of night.

HAND

Clouds darken the plain.

From all sides, the mountains of the horizon move forward; the plain shrinks, crumpled into valleys that grow deeper. The three rivers become torrents that flow swiftly in their cavernous beds towards those dark spots where they meet: the cities.

Then the sun again.

The mountains move back to the distant circular horizon; the valleys disappear, and the three rivers flow placidly in their scarcely perceptible beds of luminous sands. The cities glisten with their crystal walls and the hard light is reflected from house to house along the glass streets. Men no longer drag their dark-blue shadows like long chains that rattled on the opaque cobble stones. Silence of light: frozen wines of sound. No wind stirs, sleepily coiled around the towers that are transparent stems bearing the white flowers of clouds which float, vehicles for our pure thoughts, like water-lilies on the surface of a stream until they fade into the blue depth of space.

from THE PATHOS OF HISTORY

I

On the stereoscopic screen that's here and now, the beams of past and future meet and enjoy a transitory reality. If you close your eyes, if you sleep or forget for a while to watch, if you but faint or fail to remember yesterday or to anticipate tomorrow, then nothing is real any longer, at least until you again give the show your undivided attention. The past is real as long as you see it now as a ruin, a setting for the present; the future, real only as the seed that you hold now in your hand, the seed destined to be a whole wheat-field in another time and another place.

Our mail is delivered to us each day from the past and we send our replies into the future. Each one of us lives in a different present that draws differently on yesterday and tomorrow. Only rarely do two or more of us experience simultaneously the same present, the same mixture here and now of there and then.

II

A letter dated of the Year of the Colorless Death that has not yet befallen us came today to remind me of the pathos of the future. It spoke of our present as of a distant past that had come and gone mysteriously, leaving but monumental relics that had already puzzled generations of archaeologists and curious tourists.

My correspondent, in his flight from the metropolitan centers where the great epidemic still raged, had sought refuge in a deserted area of ruins that stood in the midst of undistinguishable rubble. History-books, he writes, had taught him something about our legendary wars, our bombings of our own cities, our "scorched earth" retreats. But what he now saw bore no trace of any greater violence than that of mere time and neglect, which destroy as thoroughly, though more slowly and less surprisingly, as any catastrophe contrived by man.

With a lyrical enthusiasm that was reminiscent at times of the best pages of Volney or of Baedecker he described to me the future ruins of our law-courts, of our Main Post-Office and of the department store where I have a charge-account, sole recognizable survivors of the architectural labyrinth that we daily tread in our search for tomorrow's spending-money. In a wilderness of rubble barely concealed beneath mounds of accumulated refuse where the weeds of centuries had blossomed and withered, the towering vestiges of these three institutions still stood before his eyes, symbols of the culture of our age.

I feel that I must answer his curious missive promptly, while I can still describe a past that is no longer at all accessible to him, a present that already hovers, in his memory, on the misty brink of oblivion. Fortunately, he and I have our despair in common, our sense of doom: we speak a common language, the speech of those subversive elements that are accustomed to loneliness in a crowd and that see death and destruction where most of their contemporaries, more loyal or more sanguine, obediently dream only of amusement and profit.

Robert Alden Sanborn (1877–1966)

THE BILLIARD PLAYERS

Whisper here, and listen to the soft click of minds. Minds, playing like cats with ivory mice, red and white mice, circle the table. The white balls do as they are told, silently spoken to the red one does its best. The cats-paw mind taps the white, rolls it upon the red, goes spinning to the green-baize edge, it returns to touch the other white. The other white says, "Click," between shut teeth. Two clicks entitle the cats-paw mind to dissolve another problem.

The table has legs like Atlas. I think they would support a world, and the world need not fear, it would not fall.

The bodies of the players lie over the polished wood, press into the rubber-cushioned inner edge, but the square legs do not bend, the hidden floor of slate does not creak complaint. There is no sound in the room above the dull grave tones of the referee, "one," "two," or, "not frozen" followed by the whispered, "Thank God," of a player as he swings his cue to the next shot.

Precise quick feet slur over the rug under the table. They pause, and over the hot silence the ivory balls pronounce resistant sounds softly, and then lie patterned as the mind, poised behind the tapering wand, designs. They catch, each one of three, a cup of light from the hanging shaded lamps, and wait for orders.

A long, long time the balls play to one tune-maker. The cue glances up into the light, delivers the pointing thrust, the wand slips back, the butt negligently brushes the nap of the rug, rises again as thought wells up in the mind, the long shaft levels under the light, the chalky pad on the tip impels the white glove upon a secret errand, the ball spins to the next one, transfers its secret and, losing speed, pauses to kiss the red. A studied hurry of the three, and they wait on the green cloth to gleam and rest, white and red and white, patterned by thought.

"One, two," and, "one hundred and one, two," so many patterns formed, disturbed, and hastening balls creasing the still air in disappearing lines and angles. The silent heated air keeps the intricate patterns within its secret archives.

One hundred and sixteen patterns the mind thinks, and puts upon the lit green floor of the table. So long as each one is accurately complete, it dissolves into another. The one hundred and seventeenth pattern is not finished. The white ball is disappointed and passes the other white without a sign. The player steals away. A match spurts red, a cigarette flourishes a streamer of blue smoke. The plotting mind of the other player circles the table, and puts his patterns upon it. "One, two."

Under his curling forefinger the cue slips smoothly one or two sufficient inches, the thumb pivots on the green surface, the other fingers keep the balance. In the fingers of the right hand the butt hangs lightly as light, swings into the shot. He builds, this man, the patterns are not so soon brushed away, his mind stands still longer, his vision is less abstract. "One, two," he plods, ploughing up hill. "One, two," the other flickers on the light wings. Like a swallow you lose sight of him, and like a swallow he brushes the common ground on his return.

"Are you sure?" the spot might ask the one. "Whither?" the white might ask the other.

AT THE ELITE

The raspberry cream melts in my mouth, dragging down to the roots of my tongue the savor of false violets.

In my left hand I hold a copy of the *Review*, high over the mound of pink lather in the silver cup. My falling eyes graze the print, and the savor of Wyndham Lewis melts down to the roots of my brain.

(As I read there is a slight arresting contraction of the nerves under the stomach, caused by the fear that the cashier is watching lest I dart out the door without paying.)

There is a hush over the room, the hush of many frosted cakes waiting for appetites. Most people are at home. This is not home. It is more peaceful.

There is also the hush of your absent presence, the fluent curves of your tenderness, which the air, this chair, and I, remember.

ALLEYS

Evening is the time to look for alleys and a wet evening is better than a dry one. They are not vulnerable by daylight, their tails are not visible, the best of salt would be useless. They are like a certain bug I know by sight, when touched with the finger of daybreak they curve into a hard grey sphere like a seed of themselves, with differentiation perfectly concealed.

I can love a street as I love a dog. Coming from the stillness of a room or the papery accumulations of an office, I delight in the doggy collisions of other people, the murmurous champing of feet on stone. The street leaps upon me, breast-high, rampant, its greedy eyes lick at my face, I feel its heavy paws upon my body. But when night falls and the dog-like street curls down on the hearthstone of the setting sun, I look about for the cat. And apart front the quivering sleep of the street, in the privacy of darkened corner, I find the small shadowy hush of an alley.

Then I need no salt to catch my alley, my fingers are not rude with daylight, they are suede-gloved with shadow. I can pick the alley up in my hands, it is limp and drowsy and unsuspecting. I can lay it down in a cushioned nook of memory, and still it lies.

Perhaps at the bottom of the alley is the face of a house, white as sand in the light of a single gas-lamp, and on the house is a green door like a pebble on the sand, and on the brick walls of the alley are dull gleams, tinged red, and patterns of mossy shadow that change. If a figure wavers up the alley like a reflection in stagnant water, it belongs there always, and goes where the alley goes, with me.

Sometimes the lone light is like a weary eye, warmed and rested by a lamp, turned low. Its slow rays rest upon the bricks or stone cobbles tenderly, a mother could not shed her love more gently on a sleeping child.

There should never be more than one light in an alley. If there are more, each one should be lonely and dim. There may be a few lighted windows, like square orange lilies lying on the surface of the shadow. If there is too much light it is not a perfect alley, nor a useful street, but something to pass without interruption. Lights must not intrude on this essential, that a true alley is an interval between uneasy facts, when you look within it you feel that you must pause and be still. Thus you may know it.

When the lights are out, the alley has gone to bed, with the sun. Drays may bump upon the cobbles, voices stab and scrape, during the day the alley will not wake. Its feline nature crouches under the rain of blatant use, and remains the feline nature.

Trees may become allied, but they are best on the further side of a wall. Then let the branches fringe the sandstone cap and paint leafy patterns on the bricks which the wind blurs foolishly. Let the gas-lamp blossom amongst the leaves. That is acceptable.

Poke about with your eyes amongst the alley things, if you like. The alley is pleased with that. But be gentle. If the alley stirs it is but to know how sweet to taste is the glutinous broth of sleep, and to carry the taste slowly away into forgetfulness. Finger the front of that tumbled old shop, caress the blackened window frames, dabble in the soot of that overhead shadow. Dirt and grime are lovely as dusk, the smell of must and mud is a flower sweetness. Do you think so? Do you know and love your alley?

If the still waters are too far for me to be led by them, I will pray beside the stillness of an alley. I have no fear in that valley of shadow.

Gertrude Stein (1874–1946)

A PIANO

If the speed is open, if the color is careless, if the selection of a strong scent is not awkward, if the button holder is held by all the waving color and there is no color, not any color. If there is no dirt in a pin and there can be none scarcely, if there is not then the place is the same as up standing.

This is no dark custom and it even is not acted in any such a way that a restraint is not spread. That is spread, it shuts and it lifts and awkwardly not awkwardly the centre is in standing.

IN BETWEEN

In between a place and candy is a narrow foot-path that shows more mounting than anything, so much really that a calling meaning a bolster measured a whole thing with that. A virgin a whole virgin is judged made and so between curves and outlines and real seasons and more out glasses and a perfectly unprecedented arrangement between old ladies and mild colds there is no satin wood shining

A SOUND

Elephant beaten with candy and little pops and chews all bolts and reckless reckless rats, this is this.

SUPPOSE AN EYES

Suppose it is within a gate which open is open at the hour of closing summer that is to say it is so.

All the seats are needing blackening. A white dress is in sign. A soldier a real soldier has a worn lace a worn lace of different sizes that is to say if he can read, if he can read he is a size to show shutting up twenty-four.

Go red go red, laugh white.

Suppose a collapse in rubbed purr, in rubbed purr get.

Little sales ladies little sales ladies little saddles of mutton.

Little sales of leather and such beautiful beautiful, beautiful beautiful.

A LONG DRESS

What is the current that makes machinery, that makes it crackle, what is the current that presents a long line and a necessary waist. What is this current.

What is the wind, what is it.

Where is the serene length, it is there and a dark place is not a dark place, only a white and red are black, only a yellow and green are blue, a pink is scarlet, a bow is every color. A line distinguishes it. A line just distinguishes it.

COLORED HATS

Colored hats are necessary to show that curls are worn by an addition of blank spaces, this makes the difference between single lines and broad stomachs, the least thing is lightening, the least thing means a little flower and a big delay a big delay that makes more nurses than little women really little women. So clean is a light that nearly all of it shows pearls and little ways. A large hat is tall and me and all custard whole.

A SUBSTANCE IN A CUSHION

The change of color is likely and a difference a very little difference is prepared. Sugar is not a vegetable.

Callous is something that hardening leaves behind what will be soft if there is a genuine interest in there being present as many girls as men. Does this change. It shows that dirt is clean when there is a volume.

A cushion has that cover. Supposing you do not like to change, supposing it is very clean that there is no change in appearance, supposing that there is regularity and a costume is that any the worse than an oyster and an exchange. Come to season that is there any extreme use in feather and cotton. Is there not much more joy in a table and more chairs and very likely roundness and a place to put them.

A circle of fine card board and a chance to see a tassel.

What is the use of a violent kind of delightfulness if there is no pleasure in not getting tired of it. The question does not come before there is a quotation. In any kind of place there is a top to covering and it is a pleasure at any rate there is some venturing in refusing to believe nonsense. It shows what use there is in a whole piece if one uses it and it is extreme and very likely the little things could be dearer but in any case there is a bargain and if there is the best thing to do is to take it away and wear it and then be reckless be reckless and resolved on returning gratitude.

Light blue and the same red with purple makes a change. It shows that there is no mistake. Any pink shows that and very likely it is reasonable. Very likely there should not be a finer fancy present. Some increase means a calamity and this is the best preparation for three and more being together. A little calm is so ordinary and in any case there is sweetness and some of that.

A seal and matches and a swan and ivy and a suit.

A closet, a closet does not connect under the bed. The band if it is white and black, the band has a green string. A sight a whole sight and a little groan grinding makes a trimming such a sweet singing trimming and a red thing no a round thing but a white thing, a red thing and a white thing.

The disgrace is not in carelessness nor even in sewing it comes out out of the way.

What is the sash like. The sash is not like anything mustard it is not like a same thing that has stripes, it is not even more hurt than that, it has a little top.

Jean Toomer (1894–1967)

CALLING JESUS

Her soul is like a little thrust-tailed dog that follows her, whimpering. She is large enough, I know, to find a warm spot for it. But each night when she comes home and closes the big outside storm door, the little dog is left in the vestibule, filled with chills till morning. Some one . . . eoho Jesus . . . soft as a cotton boll brushed against the milk-pod cheek of Christ, will steal in and cover it that it need not shiver, and carry it to her where she sleeps upon clean hay cut in her dreams.

When you meet her in the daytime on the streets, the little dog keeps coming. Nothing happens at first, and then, when she has forgotten the streets and alleys and the large house where she goes to bed of nights, a soft thing like fur begins to rub your limbs, and you hear a low, scared voice, lonely, calling, and you know that a cool something nozzles moisture in your palms. Sensitive things like nostrils, quiver. Her breath comes sweet as honeysuckle whose pistils bear the life of coming song. And her eyes carry to where builders find no need for vestibules, for swinging on iron hinges, storm doors.

Her soul is like a little thrust-tailed dog, that follows her, whimpering. I've seen it tagging on behind her, up streets where chestnut trees flowered, where dusty asphalt had been freshly sprinkled with clean water. Up alleys where niggers sat on low door-steps before tumbled shanties and sang and loved. At night, when she comes home, the little dog is left in the vestibule, nosing the crack beneath the big storm door, filled with chills till morning. Some one . . . eoho Jesus . . . soft as the bare feet of Christ moving across bales of southern cotton, will steal in and cover it that it need not shiver, and carry it to her where she sleeps: cradled in dream-fluted cane.

RHOBERT

Rhobert wears a house, like a monstrous diver's helmet, on his head. His legs are banty-bowed and shaky because as a child he had rickets. He is way down. Rods of the house like antennae of a dead thing, stuffed, prop up in the air. He is way down. He is sinking. His house is a dead thing that weights him down. He is sinking as a diver would sink in mud should the water be drawn off. Life is a murky, wiggling, microscopic water that compresses him. Compresses his helmet and would crush it the minute that he pulled his head out. He has to keep it in. Life is water that is being drawn off.

Brother, life is water that is being drawn off.
Brother, life is water that is being drawn off.

The dead house is stuffed. The stuffing is alive. It is sinful to draw one's head out of live stuffing in a dead house. The propped-up antennae would cave in and the stuffing be strewn . . shredded life-pulp . . in the water. It is sinful to have one's own head crushed. Rhobert is an upright man whose legs are banty-bowed and shaky because as a child he had rickets. The earth is round. Heaven is a sphere that surrounds it. Sink where you will. God is a Red Cross man with a dredge and a respiration-pump who's waiting for you at the opposite periphery. God built the house. He blew His breath into its stuffing. It is good to die obeying Him who can do these things.

A futile something like the dead house wraps the live stuffing of the question: how long before the water will be drawn off? Rhobert does not care. Like most men who wear monstrous helmets, the pressure it exerts is enough to convince him of its practical infinity. And he cares not two straws as to whether or not he will ever see his wife and children again. Many a time he's seen them drown in his dreams and has kicked about joyously in the mud for days after. One thing about him goes straight to the heart. He has an Adam's-apple which strains sometimes as if he were painfully gulping great globules of air . . air floating shredded life-pulp. It is a sad thing to see a banty-bowed, shaky, ricket-legged man straining the raw insides of his throat against smooth air. Holding furtive thoughts about the glory of pulp-heads strewn in water . . He is way down. Down. Mud, coming to his banty knees, almost hides them. Soon people will be looking at him and calling him a strong man. No doubt he is for one who has had rickets. Lets give it to him. Lets call him great when the water shall have been all drawn off. Lets build a monument and set it in the ooze where he goes down. A monument of hewn oak, carved in nigger-heads. Lets open our throats, brother, and sing "Deep River" when he goes down.

Brother, Rhobert is sinking.
Lets open our throats, brother,
Lets sing Deep River when he goes down.

KARINTHA

Her skin is like dusk on the eastern horizon,
O cant you see it, O cant you see it,
Her skin is like dusk on the eastern horizon
. . . When the sun goes down.

Men had always wanted her, this Karintha, even as a child, Karintha carrying beauty, perfect as dusk when the sun goes down. Old men rode her hobby-horse upon their knees. Young men danced with her at frolics when they should have been dancing with their grown-up girls. God grant us youth, secretly prayed the old men. The young fellows counted the time to pass before she would be old enough to mate with them. This interest of the male, who wishes to ripen a growing thing too soon, could mean no good to her.

Karintha, at twelve, was a wild flash that told the other folks just what it was to live. At sunset, when there was no wind, and the pine-smoke from over by the sawmill hugged the earth, and you couldnt see more than a few feet in front, her sudden darting past you was a bit of vivid color, like a black bird that flashes in light. With the other children one could hear, some distance off, their feet flopping in the two-inch dust. Karintha's running was a whir. It had the sound of the red dust that sometimes makes a spiral in the road. At dusk, during the hush just after the sawmill had closed down, and before any of the women had started their supper-getting—ready songs, her voice, high-pitched, shrill, would put one's ears to itching. But no one ever thought to make her stop because of it. She stoned the cows, and beat her dog, and fought the other children. . . Even the preacher, who caught her at mischief, told himself that she was as innocently lovely as a November cotton flower. Already, rumors were out about her. Homes in Georgia are most often built on the two-room plan. In one, you cook and eat, in the other you sleep, and there love goes on. Karintha had seen or heard, perhaps she had felt her parents loving. One could but imitate one's parents, for to follow them was the way of God. She played "home" with a small boy who was not afraid to do her bidding. That started the whole thing. Old men could no longer ride her hobby-horse upon their knees. But young men counted faster.

Her skin is like dusk,
O cant you see it,
Her skin is like dusk,
When the sun goes down.

Karintha is a woman. She who carries beauty, perfect as dusk when the sun goes down. She has been married many times. Old men remind her that a few years back they rode her hobby-horse upon their knees. Karintha smiles, and indulges them when she is in the mood for it. She has contempt for them. Karintha is a woman. Young men run stills to make her money. Young men go to the big cities and run on the road. Young men go away to college. They all want to bring her money. These are the young men who thought that all they had to do was to count time. But Karintha is a woman, and she has had a child. A child fell out of her womb onto a bed of pine-needles in the forest. Pine-needles are smooth and sweet. They are elastic to the feet of rabbits. . . A sawmill was nearby. Its pyramidal sawdust pile smoldered. It is a year before one completely burns. Meanwhile, the smoke curls up and hangs in odd wraiths about the trees, curl up, and spreads itself out over the valley. . . Weeks after Karintha returned home the smoke was so heavy you tasted it in water. Some one made a song:

> Smoke is on the hills. Rise up.
> Smoke is on the hills, O rise
> And take my soul to Jesus.

Karintha is a woman. Men do not know that the soul of her was a growing thing ripened too soon. They will bring their money; they will die not having found it out. . . Karintha at twenty, carrying beauty, perfect as dusk when the sun goes down. Karintha. . .

> Her skin is like dusk on the eastern horizon,
> O cant you see it, O cant you see it,
> Her skin is like dusk on the eastern horizon
> . . . When the sun goes down.

Goes down. . .

Thornton Wilder (1897–1975)

SENTENCES

I

In the Italian quarter of London I found a group of clerks, waiters and idealistic barbers calling itself The Rosicrucian Mysteries, Soho Chapter, that met to read papers on the fabrication of gold and its metaphysical implications, to elect from its number certain Arch-adepts and *magistri hieraticorum*, to correspond with the last of the magi, Orzinda-mazda, on Mt. Sinai, and to retell, wide-eyed, their stories of how some workmen near Rome, breaking by chance into the tomb of Cicero's daughter, Tulliola, discovered an ever-burning lamp suspended in mid-air, its wick feeding on Perpetual Principle; of how Cleopatra's son Caesarion was preserved in a translucent liquid, "oil of gold," and could be still seen in an underground shrine at Vienna ; and of how Virgil never died, but was alive still on the Island of Patmos, eating the leaves of a peculiar tree.

II

In Rome I encountered a number of people who for one reason or another were unable to sleep between midnight and dawn, and when I tossed sleepless, or when I returned late to my rooms through the deserted streets—at the hour when the parricide feels a cat purring about his feet in the darkness—I pictured to myself old Baldassare in the Borgo, former Bishop of Shantung and Apostolic Visitor to the Far East, rising at two to study with streaming eyes the Fathers and the Councils, marveling, he said, at the continuous blooming of the rose-tree of Doctrine; or of Stasia, a Russian refugee who had lost the habit of sleeping after dark during her experience as nurse in the War, Stasia playing solitaire through the night and brooding over the jocose tortures to which her family had been subjected by the soldiers of Taganrog ; and of Elizabeth Grier who, like some German prince of the Eighteenth Century, owned her own band of musicians, listening the length over her long shadowed room to some new work that D'Indy had sent her, or bending over the score while her little troupe revived the overture to *Les Indes Galantes.*

William Carlos Williams (1883–1963)

THE DELICACIES

The hostess, in pink satin and blond hair—dressed high—shone beautifully in her white slippers against the great silent bald head of her little-eyed husband!

Raising a glass of yellow Rhine wine in the narrow space just beyond the light-varnished woodwork and the decorative column between dining-room and hall, she smiled the smile of water tumbling from one ledge to another.

We began with a herring salad: delicately flavored saltiness in scallops of lettuce leaves.

The little owl-eyed and thick-set lady with masses of grey hair has smooth pink cheeks without a wrinkle. She cannot be the daughter of the little red-faced fellow dancing about inviting lion headed Wolff the druggist to play the piano! But she is. Wolff is a terrific smoker: if the telephone goes off at night—so his curled-haired wife whispers—he rises from bed but cannot answer till he has lighted a cigarette.

Sherry wine in little conical glasses, dull brownish yellow, and tomatoes stuffed with finely cut chicken and mayonnaise!

The tall Irishman in a Prince Albert and the usual striped trousers is going to sing for us. (The piano is in a little alcove with dark curtains.) The hostess's sister—ten years younger than she—in black net and velvet, has hair like some filmy haystack, cloudy about the eyes. She will play for her husband.

My wife is young, yes she is young and pretty when she cares to be—when she is interested in a discussion: it is the little dancing mayor's wife telling her of the Day nursery in East Rutherford, 'cross the track, divided from us by the railroad—and disputes as to precedence. It is in this town the saloon flourishes, the saloon of my friend on the right whose wife has twice offended with chance words. Her English is atrocious! It is in this town that the saloon is situated, close to the railroad track, close as may be, this side being dry, dry, dry: two people listening on opposite sides of a wall!—The Day Nursery had sixty-five babies the week before last, so my wife's eyes shine and her cheeks are pink and I cannot see a blemish.

Ice-cream in the shape of flowers and domestic objects: a pipe for me since I do not smoke, a doll for you.

The figure of some great bulk of a woman disappearing into the kitchen with a quick look over the shoulder. My friend on the left who has spent the whole day in a car the like of which some old fellow would give to an actress: flower-holders, mirrors, curtains, plush seats—my friend on the left who is chairman of the Streets committee of the town council—and who has spent the whole day studying automobile fire-engines in neighboring towns in view of purchase,—my friend, at the Elks last week at the breaking-up hymn, signaled for them to let Bill—a familiar friend of the saloon-keeper—sing out all alone to the organ—and he did sing!

Salz-rolls, exquisite! and Rhine wine *ad libitum*. A masterly caviar sandwich.

The children flitting about above stairs. The councilman has just bought a National eight—some car!

For heaven's sake I mustn't forget the halves of green peppers stuffed with cream cheese and whole walnuts!

from KORA IN HELL: IMPROVISATIONS

III

I

So far away August green as it yet is. They say the sun still comes up o'mornings and it's harvest moon now. Always one leaf at the peak twig swirling, swirling and apples rotting in the ditch.

2

My wife's uncle went to school with Amundsen. After he, Amundsen, returned from the south pole there was a Scandinavian dinner, which bored Amundsen like a boyhood friend. There was a young woman at his table, silent and aloof from the rest. She left early and he restless at some impalpable delay apologized suddenly and went off with two friends, his great, lean bulk twitching agilely. One knew why the poles attracted him. Then my wife's mother told me the same old thing, how a girl in their village jilted him years back. But the girl at the supper ! Ah—that comes later when we are wiser and older.

3

What can it mean to you that a child wears pretty clothes and speaks three languages or that its mother goes to the best shops? It means : July has good need of his blazing sun. But if you pick one berry from the ash tree I'd not know it again for the same no matter how the rain washed. Make my bed of witchhazel twigs, said the old man, since they bloom on the brink of winter.

———————

There is neither beginning nor end to the imagination but it delights in its own seasons reversing the usual order at will. Of the air of the coldest room it will seem to build the hottest passions. Mozart would dance with his wife, whistling his own tune to keep the cold away and Villon ceased to write upon his Petit Testament only when the ink was frozen. But men in the direst poverty of the imagination buy finery and indulge in extravagant moods in order to piece out their lack with other matter.

XIII

I

Their half sophisticated faces gripe me in the belly. There's no business to be done with them either way. They're neither virtuous nor the other thing, between which exist no perfections. Oh, the mothers will explain that they are good girls. But these never guess that there's more sense in a sentence heard backward than forward most times. A country whose flowers are without perfume and whose girls lack modesty—the saying goes—. Dig deeper *mon ami*, the rock maidens are running naked in the dark cellars.

———————————

In disgust at the spectacle of an excess of ripe flesh that, in accordance with the local custom of the place he is in, will be left to wither without ever achieving its full enjoyment, a young man of the place consoles himself with a vision of perfect beauty.

2

I'll not get it no matter how I try. Say it was a girl in black I held open a street door for. Let it go at that. I saw a man an hour earlier I liked better much better. But it's not so easy to pass over. Perfection's not a thing you'll let slip so easily. What a body. The little flattened buttocks ; the quiver of the flesh under the smooth fabric ! Agh, it isn't that I want to go to bed with you. In fact what is there to say? except the mind's a queer nereid sometimes and flesh is at least as good a gauze as words are : something of that. Something of mine—yours—hearts on sleeves? Ah *zut* what's the use? It's not that I've lost her again either. It's hard to tell loss from gain anyway.

3

The words of the thing twang and twitter to the gentle rocking of a high-laced boot and the silk above that. The trick of the dance is in following now the words, *allegro*, now the contrary beat of the glossy leg : Reaching far over as if—But always she draws back and comes down upon the word flat footed. For a moment we—but the boot's costly and the play's not mine. The pace leads off anew. Again the words break it and we both come down flatfooted. Then—near the knee, jumps to the eyes, catching in the hair's shadow. But the lips take the rhythm again and again we come down flatfooted. By this time boredom takes a hand and the play's ended.

A MATISSE

On the french grass, in that room on Fifth Ave., lay that woman who had never seen my own poor land. The dust and noise of Paris had fallen from her with the dress and underwear and shoes and stockings which she had just put aside to lie bathing in the sun. So too she lay in the sunlight of the man's easy attention. His eye and the sun had made day over her. She gave herself to them both for there was nothing to be told. Nothing is to be told to the sun at noonday. A violet clump before her belly mentioned that it was spring. A locomotive could be heard whistling beyond the hill. There was nothing to be told. Her body was neither classic nor whatever it might be supposed. There she lay and her curving torso and thighs were close upon the grass and violets.

So he painted her. The sun had entered his head in the color of sprays of flaming palm leaves. They had been walking for an hour or so after leaving the train. They were hot. She had chosen the place to rest and he had painted her resting, with interest in the place she had chosen.

It had been a lovely day in the air.—What pleasant women are these girls of ours! When they have worn clothes and take them off it is with an effect of having performed a small duty. They return to the sun with a gesture of accomplishment. —Here she lay in this spot today not like Diana or Aphrodite but with better proof than they of regard for the place she was in. She rested and he painted her.

It was the first of summer. Bare as was his mind of interest in anything save the fullness of his knowledge, into which her simple body entered as into the eye of the sun himself, so he painted her. So she came to America.

No man in my country has seen a woman naked and painted her as if he knew anything except that she was naked. No woman in my country is naked except at night.

In the french sun, on the french grass in a room on Fifth Ave., a french girl lies and smiles at the sun without seeing us.

THEESSENTIALROAR

It is the roar first brilliantly overdone THEN the plug in the pipe that carries them home with a ROAR and a cigarette and a belly full of sweet sugar and the roar of the film or to sit at the busy hour in the polished window of Union Club at the northeast corner of fifty-first street across the street from St. Patrick's (so to speak) neat gray catholic cathedral and feel the roar pleasantly pricking the face but they're all face as the Indian said to Ben Franklin who also knew French women like the New York Journal which knows that unless it roars it does not do the trick and that's the trick that you have to have the money for like Weissmuller when he slaps the mater with his hands, quick, the way they talk and THAT's what makes them WIN, it just HAPPENS but when a baby drops a ball of twine and it rolllllllls unwinding about their feet neatly semicolon placed in rows while the cigar train is sucked at by the throat of the tube and it rolls without WITHOUT any roar at all along among the feet everybody smiles because it DOES something to everybody it SURPRISES them all because it SHOWS UP the roar and nice colored men smile and a nice fat man picks it up and a very nice lady smiles like the translation of a norse saga that the sea has left when the plug slips through the pipe, the toss and danger of the cold sea is dead in English keeps them kidded so the emptiness of the continent has been filled, that's the crowd at the door jamming and pushing both ways, YOUNG hit a ball with a stick stick to it roar out around the middle its the brush hedge on which the vine leans hell with booze who can't invent noise that carries a rock drill in its breeches WHOOP it up and we'll ride the bronk with the hands tied ka plunk ka plunk opens up the old clam under your ribs till the whisky of it tickles the capillaries around the fissure of Sylvius and the milky way weigh spits out a drop or two of fire to you? I'm just too lazy like when he got the capsicum vaseline on the finger of his glove when he was making the regional examination and the result was SURPRISING.

from FOR BILL BIRD

It was getting kinda late. We'd been talking cars. I wanted them to come in on a new model we had just unloaded. He seemed interested but she wouldn't let him buy it. So I kept talking, stalling along hoping for a break.

Pretty soon I hears a car pull up in front of the house and stop. I thought someone was coming in. I waited a while then I ast them if they'd heard it too.

Oh, yes, she says, that's our daughter coming home from the movies.

That was all right but after another half hour and nobody comin in I spoke up again. I guess you were wrong, I says, about that being your daughter.

No, she says, she usually sits out there with her boy friend for a while before coming in. I suppose she sees the light and knows we're up.

A little after twelve o'clock the car starts up and I could hear it wade down the street. Then someone comes runnin up the front steps. The door flings open and in comes the girl. A peach, take it from me. As soon as she sees me she stops and stands there swinging her panties around on the finger tips of her left hand.

Hello folks, she says then, and lets her underwear go onto a couch. How's everybody?

Evelyn! says her mother, I hope you're not going to bring disgrace and scandal into this house.

Oh don't worry, Mother, she says, we're careful.

VERBAL TRANSCRIPTION—6 A.M.

The Wife:

About an hour ago. He woke up and it was as if a knife was sticking in his side. I tried the old reliable, I gave him a good drink of whisky but this time it did no good. I thought it might be his heart so I . . . Yes. In between his pains he was trying to get dressed. He could hardly stand up but through it all he was trying to get himself ready to go to work. Can you imagine that?

Rags! Leave the man alone. The minute you're good to him he . . . Look at him sitting up and begging! Rags! Come here! Do you want to look out of the window? Oh, yes. That's his favorite amusement—like the rest of the family. And we're not willing just to look out. We have to lean out as if we were living on Third Avenue.

Two dogs killed our old cat last week. He was thirteen years old. That's unusual for a cat, I think. We never let him come upstairs. You know he was stiff and funny looking. But we fed him and let him sleep in the cellar. He was deaf and I suppose he couldn't fight for himself and so they killed him.

Yes. We have quite a menagerie. Have you seen our bluejay? He had a broken wing. We've had him two years now. He whistles and answers us when we call him. He doesn't look so good but he likes it here. We let him out of the cage sometimes with the window open. He goes to the sill and looks out. Then he turns and runs for his cage as if he was scared. Sometimes he sits on the little dog's head and they are great friends. If he went out I'm afraid he wouldn't understand and they would kill him too.

And a canary. Yes. You know I was afraid it was his heart. Shall I dress him now? This is the time he usually takes the train to be there at seven o'clock. Pajamas are so cold. Here put on this old shirt—this old horse blanket, I always call it. I'm sorry to be such a fool but those needles give me a funny feeling all over. I can't watch you give them. Thank you so much for coming so quickly. I have a cup of coffee for you all ready in the kitchen.

THE PACE THAT KILLS

No, thanks, I said, as he offered me a cigarette. That's right, he said, you're not smoking. He told you that yesterday, interposed his wife.

Well, sir, he continued glancing sidewise at her, you don't mind if I . . . ? Not at all. Have you got a match? Yes, right here. I enjoy it. And it doesn't seem to hurt me. You ought to have seen this place last night. We didn't get to bed till after one this morning. The air was blue with it.

You old fellows are tougher than we modern weaklings. I can't take it any more.

Yes, I'm getting along I guess, he went on. Why, one of the girls last night was looking at a few daguerreotypes we have here. She didn't know whether they were tintypes or what they were. And I told her, you young people take everything for granted, automobiles, airplanes, telephones, even electric lights. You act as if they've always been here. You don't mean to tell me, she said, that you remember when there were no electric lights? She didn't want to believe me.

So I told her I remembered when they had the first electric lights at the Centennial Exhibition in Philadelphia in '76. We were little children, of course, but I remember it. It was just a toy then. Nobody thought it would ever amount to anything.

Yes, I said, even I can remember when Pop swore he wouldn't have a telephone in the house. Why, he used to say, your privacy will be gone forever after that. How right he was.

Sit down—my old friend really had got hold of something this time—sit down if you have a minute, said he, and I'll tell you something you'll hardly believe. His wife in her easy chair smiled but didn't open her mouth, she the easy, stable one, he the voluble, active one of the pair.

J. G. Geoghan, of East Orange. I don't know what he is now, President of some big corporation in New York. He was the first manager for the Newark Telephone Co. Yes, sir, the first manager. And he's still alive and active.

Just a few years ago he had facsimiles made of the first sub-scriber list, the year the exchange opened. He distributed them around among some of his acquaintances. I had one—but it's gone now. It may be around somewhere but anyhow it's gone.

It was a card, maybe eight by ten inches or so and it had on it two columns of names, maybe fifty names. Just the names, mind you, that's all, no numbers. That was the Newark Telephone Directory. So that when you wanted to call up somebody in Newark you asked for Mr. So and So. What do you think of that? Just a few years ago. And look at the size of it today.

Yes, sir. Time moves, I said. But our lives become shorter and shorter.

In one short lifetime all those chances, and that's only one thing.

Yes, it adds up but it doesn't multiply. No wonder we've gone nuts, huh?

EXULTATION

The rain surpasses itself. It has gone beyond itself to the contours of a happy day. A day of sunshine, a June day, a day when the old gardener is arrested by a scent of roses wakens to the small sounds of the driving rain.

It is a weekend holiday the first of the year in the good weather, when everyone has gone to the lake. The cottage has to be cleaned, the windows opened, the roof, broken by last February's ice storm, repaired. The mice that have built a nest in the rags back of the kitchen door, routed. But it is too lovely to spend all our time indoors.

Bill is in the garden. "Come on out, Daphne, and look at this sky and this water. It does something to you. It really does!" He has been raking dead oak leaves from the almost buried arena of the summer's anticipated operations for leisure and going back and forth: to the float, back entry. Everything has to be cleared and put in order.

The rain continues to fall. It penetrates to the bones. This dampness and this chill is a foretaste of the grave.

But it is in the rain, the rain, friend of the seeds, friend of all budding things that in the microscopy of its attention puts my dejection to shame. Without the rain—without this rain, without this dejection, the humor of the quicksilver lizard would not inhabit the breathing sand. He scampers, his throat, as he lifts his head to watch me, pulsing rapidly. I shift my eyes and he is gone.

Which is he?

If he is not the rain, what is he? In the microscopy of its attention exists also a pulse of oars, the slow dip and withdrawal. And the talk. And the intent of the talk. And the silences. The slow forward and back. The smell of the fishy lakewater. The heat of the day. The shores equidistant from the shallow boat as it moves in leisurely fashion upon the hardly rippled lake. There are the cries of the splashing children swimming at the place set aside for them.

The time is ripe. Now is the time. There is no other time in which to exult at the brilliant fulfillment of a summer day.

AFTERWORD: SUPPLE AND JARRING

> What is poetry and if you know what poetry is
> what is prose.
>
> —Gertrude Stein, "Poetry and Grammar"

For years I wrote prose poems without knowing what I was doing, thinking instead that I was writing some sort of shrunken, deformed story that I was too lazy to transform into a piece of *real* fiction. At the time, *prose poem* to me meant some sort of Dadaesque stream-of-consciousness vignette—and I, on the other hand, was writing what I thought of simply as very short stories. (Often I would write in the third person, for example, a staple of fiction but a point of view rarely used in lyric poetry, John Berryman's *Dream Songs* notwithstanding.) This was long before the term *flash* had been applied to fiction in any but a marketing sense, and *short shorts* still referred to an item of clothing.

For a while I told anyone who would listen that I was writing, or attempting to write, "experimental fiction." While it was true that these pieces, put together as a sequence, did hint at an underlying theme, a montage-like connection of some sort between the disparate sections, in a traditional sense they lacked pretty much all semblance of a plot. So it wasn't long before I felt uncomfortable calling them fiction at all and began writing sentences which were broken up into lines—that is, *free verse*. But this wasn't satisfying either. I kept feeling self-conscious, as though the words I was putting on the page were announcing themselves as POETRY—and I had to keep thinking of how and where to end the line, or of how

229

it would seem if I didn't end it but instead began to sound like Blake or Whitman or Ginsberg. No, that wasn't what I wanted at all. I wanted to write *prose*, thank you very much.

One day, I decided to come out of the closet and to admit that, Yes, I was writing prose poems—but then to add, *sotto voce:* Though perhaps they're not what you've come to think of as prose poems. I wasn't sure at the time that many people in America had come to think much at all about the prose poem, but by God I knew what I thought of it. It gave me the freedom to play with a mix of characteristics of tone and style and subject matter that were traditionally the realm of fiction writers, along with other elements that were traditionally poetic. That was the key to me: to be able to draw on the resources available to both fiction writers and poets.

> What I was searching for was a medium in which I could say anything I wanted—which for poets is something like finding the philosopher's stone or the elixir vitae. For one thing, I wanted to be able to use the ridiculous, for another the nonsensical, for another the "obscene." I wanted to be as personal as I liked, as autobiographical when I felt like it, editorializing or pompous, in short, to be able to drop into any intensity of language at any time. None of this was particularly original, but it was new to me.[1]

Contrary to what this statement by Karl Shapiro might suggest, there was at that time a widespread prejudice against the prose poem, an attitude that saw in the form a less-than-savory immigrant from overseas, which in the words of one critic brought "a visitation of collective ungiftedness." The reviewer in this case, W. M. Spackman, goes on to say that prose poetry is "a genre whose spiritual inconveniences it takes very tough creative discipline to stand up under"—and "one of those accidents of French rhetoric . . . that the French take to be literature."[2] Confronted by this attitude, I embarked on a personal mission to justify the ways of the prose poem to poets and critics alike.

When I began the research that led to this anthology, I thought I already knew a great deal about the history of the form. I knew, for example, about the French *poème en prose* that had originated in the nineteenth century—out of the wreckage, as it were, of Chateaubriand's prose epics—about Aloysius Bertrand and Charles Baudelaire and those who followed them. Across the English Channel I was familiar with a tradition of prose poetry that started, one might say, with the King James Bible, and which continued on to the Aesthetes and beyond. In America I knew about Whitman's *Specimen Days,* and I thought I had a sense of the variety of more recent work, from Gertrude Stein's *Tender Buttons* and William Carlos Williams' *Kora in Hell* to Robert Bly's *Morning Glory.* From the Beats I knew, for example, Ginsberg's "Supermarket in California" and Diane di Prima's *Dinners & Nightmares.* I knew about Russell Edson's incomparable little stories, and Kenneth Patchen's fables. I had read to the point of exhaustion Michael Benedikt's *The Prose Poem: An International Anthology,* and I thought I had the bases pretty much covered.

This was back in the dark ages of information technology. My most advanced piece of equipment was an IBM "selectric" typewriter, and for research I depended on the card catalog of the University of Wisconsin Memorial Library and the cumbersome volumes of the OCLC Union Catalog, still many years away from being available online—"online" itself being many years away. But there was one other resource that I was fortunate enough to have just a few miles from my apartment, and that was the University of Wisconsin Memorial Library rare book department—and in particular, the Little Magazine Collection. When I arrived in the rare book reading room that September day, I thought that the modern American prose poem, Stein and Williams notwithstanding, could be dated primarily from the publication, in 1964, of Russell Edson's *The Very Thing That Happens.* After that, for whatever reason, little magazines began to publish prose poems in much greater quantity than previously. A decade later, Michael Benedikt became poetry editor of the *Paris Review* and shortly thereafter his groundbreaking anthology appeared. By the end of the seventies, the prose poem had become, in Donald Hall's words, "a dominant American literary form."[3]

Digging deeper, I found Charles Henri Ford's "Little Anthology of the Poem in Prose," published in *New Directions* 14 in 1953. When I came across this mini-anthology, with a whole different cast of characters, I knew I had a lot more reading to do. Over the course of the next few months, I discovered an accumulation of American prose poems from the first half of the twentieth century so extensive that it deserved in my mind to be called a tradition, or at least the beginnings of one.

In the early years of the twentieth century, two cities in the United States, New York and Chicago, were developing as centers of modernist activity in the arts. This was the era of the Armory Show of 1913, and in particular of Marcel Duchamp's *Nude Descending a Staircase*—explosive, liberating, and scandalous in certain quarters of the art world—marking in retrospect a watershed moment, signaling a complete break with the past. As Gertrude Stein remarked later, a new era had dawned even before the First World War "made its ending official."[4] Gravitating at first around these two poles, a movement arose among a group of writers to create a specifically *modern* and specifically *American* literature. For Sherwood Anderson, this meant a desire to write not in the language of books but in "the language of the streets, of American towns and cities, the language of the factories and warehouses . . . the saloons, the farms." It was a revolt that held as its enemy the Genteel Tradition of New England:

> Anyway, there we were, intellectually dominated by New England. . . . We wanted to escape from it. We all were in revolt. Our land was not the New England land. The soil in our fields was black and rich. It went deep. The corn in our fields grew like forest trees. . . . I worked out my own *Mid-American Chants* in an attempt to sing smoke-laden city streets, great corn fields, the barnyards of our farmers, their great horses, the mud-banks of our rivers flowing sluggishly under their bridges.[5]

It's all too easy from the distance of a hundred years, now that conversational American English has long been accepted into poetry, to overlook this aspect of home-grown Modernism.

"The resistance was against the established English language," Kay Boyle tells us, "and the fight was for the recognition of a new American tongue."[6]

"We do not speak English—remember that," adds William Carlos Williams: "We speak our own language." And furthermore: "Let speech be the rule."[7]

If not iambic itself, free verse plays itself off against the deeply-felt iambic rhythm of blank verse, the other unrhymed verse in English—and is haunted by its ghost. Though it works for British intonations, it's difficult to render the cadence of American speech in an iambic line, and for this reason the prose poem serves historically as a vehicle for the development of an American poetic voice—released from the long shadow that blank verse casts over English *vers libre*.

So What *Is* a Prose Poem, and Where Did It Come From?

A prose poem, on its face, is a page or two of writing that looks like any other prose—that is, single columns whose lines go out to the edge of the page, and where no aural or visual significance should be attributed to the line-breaks. As Russell Edson tells us,

> Superficially a prose poem should look somewhat like a page from a child's primer, indented paragraph beginnings, justified margins. In other words the prose poem should not announce that it is a special prose: if it is,

the reader will know it. The idea is to get away from obvious ornament, and the obligations implied therein.[8]

This is not a new form: the fable and parable have a firmly-established position in world literature, dating to antiquity. One of William Caxton's first books printed in English, in the late fifteenth century, was just such a collection, *The Fables of Alphonse of Poggio*—and chapbooks of one sort or another, many containing short prose pieces, appear with regularity over the next couple of hundred years.[9] In the seventeenth century, a history of the form in English would include, along with portions of the King James Bible, John Donne's and Thomas Traherne's "meditations"—and a century later, James Macpherson's fake translations from the mythical poet Ossian. Influenced perhaps by Macpherson, Blake scattered "memorable fancies," each like some lost Biblical verse, throughout his *Marriage of Heaven and Hell*; and in the early nineteenth century Leigh Hunt published slice-of-life sketches—each one of which he called a "now."[10]

In mid-nineteenth-century Paris, the poet Charles Baudelaire began writing short prose pieces which he called *petits poèmes en prose.* In a letter to the editor Arsène Houssaye, Baudelaire explains that his model for these pieces was Aloysius Bertrand's *Gaspard de la nuit* (1843), with its "strangely picturesque" prose sketches, adapted to "a modern and more abstract life."[11] "Which one of us," asks Baudelaire, "has not dreamed, in his ambitious days, of the miracle of a poetic prose . . . supple enough and jarring enough *[assez souple et assez heurtée]* to be adapted to the soul's lyrical movements, to the undulations of reverie, to the sudden starts that consciousness takes?" In his journals, Baudelaire also acknowledges his artistic debt to Alphonse Rabbe, whose collection, *L'Album d'un pessimiste* (1836), is in part a series of melancholy little sketches.[12] After Baudelaire, French literature is replete with prose poets.

Toward the end of the nineteenth century the prose poem in English literature, following the French example, becomes a well-recognized form—Oscar Wilde's "poems in prose" and Ernest Dowson's prose "decorations," for example—and it takes on the atmosphere of decadence and aestheticism by which later generations define this period and, indeed, the form itself. (It certainly didn't help the reputation of the prose poem that the term was used in open court to characterize a billet-doux that Oscar Wilde had sent his lover.) Other writers of prose poems in English from this era include John Synge and Olive Schreiner. Synge's work is particularly interesting because, while translating Petrarch's sonnets into prose, he uses the Irish vernacular. Schreiner's *Dreams*, on the other hand, though expressing her feminism, continue to use the archaic dialect of Wilde's and Dowson's work. Also included here should be Joyce's "Epiphanies," youthful neo-Symbolist pieces written between 1898 and 1904.

Over in America, in the early 1860s, Walt Whitman wrote a series of prose sketches which he titled "City Photographs," some of them focusing on New York Hospital and published pseudononymously in the New York *Leader.*[13] Starting in 1862 as a volunteer in army hospitals during the Civil War, Whitman kept detailed notes, sketches he published later as *Memoranda during the War,* and which he further expanded upon in *Specimen Days.* Though we have no evidence that Baudelaire's prose poems influenced

Whitman in any way, we do know that Lafcadio Hearn, writing in the 1880s, was familiar with them, as he quotes from one in his prose poem, "Spring Phantoms" (first published in the New Orleans *Item* in April 1881).[14] A few years later, in 1890, the poet Stuart Merrill introduces the French prose poem to a broader American audience, with his publication of the anthology *Pastels in Prose*. In his introduction, William Dean Howells speaks of the prose poem as "a peculiarly modern invention"—and he goes on to say, "I do not know the history of the French Poem in Prose, but I am sure that, as we say in our graphic slang, it has come to stay."[15]

And stay it did. Whether it's in the literary experimentation of Gelett Burgess and Porter Garnett in the San Francisco *Lark*, or the musings of of James Huneker and Vance Thompson in *Mlle New York*, or the work of the authors of the *Chap-Book* in Chicago, the *fin-de-siècle* poem-in-prose was alive and well in America. We can draw the conclusion that, as William Carlos Williams says of himself, American modernists were quite familiar with this sort of piece, if only as something from which to distinguish their own work. "I was familiar with the typically French prose poem," Williams says; "its pace was not the same as my own compositions."[16] As for the work of twentieth-century French prose poets, American writers could read it in the pages of some of the same magazines that were publishing their own work. Unfortunately, as I see it, the importance of the prose poem in France has gone a long way toward delaying the recognition of its significance in Anglo-American literature.

These days, American writing is filled with such experiments in short prose, whether they go by the name prose poem, or flash fiction, or whatever else happens to be the expression *du jour:* two fairly recent coinages, for example, being *pp/ff* and *prose block*. There is an online journal, *Brevity,* dedicated to "concise literary nonfiction." There is a journal of "prose poetics," *Sentence,* and at least one book series devoted to single-author collections of prose poems. There is a whole industry built on brief fiction, online and in print; in fact, the bibliography in the *Rose Metal Press Field Guide to Writing Flash Fiction* (2009) lists seventeen anthologies of self-identified short shorts or flash fiction published since 1982, the year I finished my doctoral work.

Historically of more recent vintage than the term poem-in-prose, the notion of flash fiction—whatever it's called—is not in fact particularly new. In 1936 there appeared a book titled *365 Days,* composed entirely of brief short stories prompted by some event from each day of the year 1934—each story, as the editors say, "all of a more or less equal length, approximately three hundred words." The editors continue, somewhat disingenuously in my opinion, "but in specifying that the stories be so compactly done we were not so much seeking an experimental vehicle as indicating necessary limits of space."[17] In fact, the Rose Metal *Field Guide* traces the first use of the term "short short story" to a 1926 issue of *Collier's Weekly.*[18]

T. S. Eliot refers to *Finnegans Wake* as "a kind of vast prose poem"—but let's be clear, that's not what this discussion is about.[19] We're talking here about a form which is to the world of prose much as a sonnet is to the world of traditional verse, that is, short and self-contained. So I do think we need, at least theoretically, a term which will encompass all such works, whether we call them fiction or poetry—a term referring only to the basic structure we're discussing, one or two pages of prose. Perhaps we can call this simply a *short*, taking our cue from Samuel Beckett, who was a writer of both stories and poems in both French and English. He was perhaps not the first to use the term, but his stature overshadows anyone else I can think of.

Here's my contention: I'd say that the human mind has an ability to grasp as a unified whole an image lying open before it—and perhaps not much more. We can "get" a single painting, but a walk through even one room of a museum presents the mind with a different sort of task altogether. There's a maximum amount of information of whatever sort, visual or textual, that we can, as the expression goes, "get our minds around"—or at least, the way our mind gets itself around something is different when only a very limited focus of time and space is necessary for a first complete impression. Two pages, a folio of a book lying open before a reader, is one sort of thing—but the whole *megillah* is something else again. The minute or two or several it takes to read through a paragraph, or several, is a span short enough that we can go back and read it again, and again, and still have it seem, as Yeats said in a related context, "a moment's thought." Certain it is that the mind can grasp a page or two of text in a way that longer texts elude. Somewhere in the neighborhood of a thousand words or less—depending in part on the reader and the time of day—the mind starts running off in various different directions. Reading short prose has its own peculiar charm.

But how short is short? In the "Philosophy of Composition,"

Edgar Allan Poe draws the following conclusion:

> If any literary work is too long to be read at one sitting, we must be content to dispense with the immensely important effect derivable from unity of impression. . . . What we term a long poem is, in fact, merely a succession of brief ones—that is to say, of brief poetical effects. . . .
>
> It appears evident, then, that there is a distinct limit, as regards length, to all works of literary art—the limit of a single sitting—and that, although in certain classes of prose composition . . . this limit may be advantageously overpassed, it can never properly be overpassed in a poem.[20]

In the years since Poe wrote, I think the attention span of the average reader has diminished—or at least the time available for reading has shrunk from competition with all other leisure-time activities. What Poe considered "a single sitting" allowed, as he said, for a hundred-line poem, more or less. Given the pace of life these days, that same chunk of attention would now encompass, I'd say, a page or two of text.

Before we can determine what it means to say that a page or two of prose can function as a poem, we need to address the fact that it's written in prose. This seems at first a tautology, that a prose poem is written in prose—but let's examine the effect that prose has on the reader, its difference from free verse. In the Rose Metal *Field Guide* to flash fiction, Steve Almond presents both a lineated and unlineated version of the same piece, "Stop."[21]

First he gives the reader the "free verse" version:

> Or maybe you're here, in Sturbridge, Mass.,
> off the pike, punching the register, Roy Rogers,
> a girl in a brown smock. America comes at you on buses,
> in caps and shorts, fuming. What the hell,
> you're killing each other, anyway.
> This kind of loneliness. What are words?
> You've got chores, duties,
> an inanimate world that needs you.
> Sometimes, late afternoon, you scrape the grill
> and figure: this could be love, this clean violence,
> the meaty shavings and steel beneath.
> There are other ideas out there, in magazines
> and movies, sweaters, perfume, your beautiful money.
> But you see your life, that which persists,
> the dumpster out back, the counter dulled
> by your hands, relish troughs to fill.
> Some days the clouds are so thick they seem weighted.
> You are kind and not especially pretty.
> You do your job. You are polite. At great expense,
> you smile. Your best friend died
> just down the road, in an accident at night.
> You laid a pink bear before the marker
> and you persisted, you persist.

And then the prose:

Or maybe you're here, in Sturbridge, Mass., off the pike, punching the register, Roy Rogers, a girl in a brown smock. America comes at you on buses, in caps and shorts, fuming. What the hell, you're killing each other, anyway. This kind of loneliness. What are words? You've got chores, duties, an inanimate world that needs you. Sometimes, late afternoon, you scrape the grill and figure: this could be love, this clean violence, the meaty shavings and steel beneath. There are other ideas out there, in magazines and movies, sweaters, perfume, bales of beautiful money. But you see your life, that which persists, the dumpster out back, the counter dulled by your hands, relish troughs to fill. Some days the clouds are so thick they seem weighted. You are kind and not especially pretty. You do your job. You are polite. At great expense, you smile. Your best friend died just down the road, in an accident at night. You laid a pink bear before the marker and you persisted, you persist.

Aside from the fact that "your beautiful money" in the lineated version changes to "bales of beautiful money" in the prose version, these two pieces are identical. But, as I read them through, they seem to me like very different pieces. I find the line breaks in the free verse jarring; the poem seems choppy and not at all "of a piece"—and on the other hand, the prose version has a seamlessness, a flow, which for me (and according to his statement, to Steve Almond as well) makes it a much more successful literary effort. Difficult as it is to put this impression into words, it's not at all difficult to sense that there is indeed a difference. Almond's use of the second person for the protagonist in this piece is also worth mentioning, as it's rare in the world of traditional narrative, though common enough in contemporary poetry and flash fiction. What's clear, in any case, is that this piece, as prose, has quite a different feel to it than when printed as free verse.

This difference is long-standing. In his disquisition on the advent of movable type and its effect on literature, H. J. Chaytor describes the growing popularity of prose long before Gutenberg enabled its cheap and easy distribution:

> Prose made its way by slow degrees, as education advanced and as people learned to read for themselves; prose versions of earlier poems began to appear at the end of the twelfth century to meet the taste of readers who wanted a story devoid of the padding and prolixity which delayed the action in the verse narratives.

And as he goes on to say,

> Prose became distinguished as dealing with matters of fact and not of fancy. . . . it became clear that a family chronicle, written in verse, would vastly gain in authority and dignity, if it were written in prose; it would, in fact, become real history.[22]

Prose, that is, purports to tell of the real world. One thing this means in practice is that the prose poem can take advantage of the conventions of all different sorts of writing—now masquerading, for example, as a journal entry or, in Vern Rutsala's words, as "a quiet parody of official prose of various kinds."[23] According to David Young,

> Most people think of the prose poem as perverse, an excuse for laziness on the part of the poet. I used to feel the same way. But in reading and teaching prose poems I learned that it was more useful to come at them from the other direction, as a distilling and mimicking of the normal ways of prose. From that perspective, interesting possibilities start to suggest themselves: life histories reduced to paragraphs, essays the size of postcards, novels in nutshells, maps on postage stamps, mind-bending laundry lists, theologies scribbled on napkins.[24]

This ability to switch diction from one register to another—this phenomenon of *heteroglossia*, to use Bakhtin's term—helps explain the special flexibility of the prose poem, a piece shifting between lyric and narrative textures.[25] The prose poem can seem to be many things (which is why I hesitate to call it a genre, as it can partake of so many), and this is the key to its ease and fluidity, to the manifold voices it can successfully project.

That a poem can be written in prose was not always obvious to many critics, perhaps foremost among them T. S. Eliot. In 1921, he finds the phenomenon puzzling:

The distinction between "verse" and "prose" is clear;
the distinction between "poetry" and "prose" is very
obscure. . . . I object to the term "prose-poetry" because
it seems to imply a sharp distinction between "poetry"
and "prose" which I do not admit, and if it does not
imply this distinction, the term is meaningless and
otiose, as there can be no combination of what is not
distinguished.[26]

Despite Eliot's confusion, it seems clear to me that *prose*, in *prose-poetry* or *prose-poem*, is used as a modifier, not as a noun. And is the distinction between *poetry* and *prose* really that obscure? As Molière's *bourgeois gentilhomme* would have it, "For more than forty years I've been speaking prose without knowing anything about it." From this point of view, the term defines everyday speech as it's written, both formal and informal—the language of the newspaper, the novel, the magazine article, the letter home. 'Poetry,' on the other hand, is a word that can be used for art or grace itself, as in the cliché made so popular by singer Johnny Tillotson. Poetry is not synonymous with verse, but rather is a state that verse can sometimes aspire to. And 'poem,' conversely, is a term that describes a specific sort of art object—that is, a word-object set upon a mental pedestal, or put into a frame, an object distinguished from everyday discourse. In a lyric poem, a lineated poem, the frame surrounding it consists of both the white space on the rest of the page and, more abstractly, the whole tradition of poetic art. If such a word-object can be written in verse, why not in prose? And as Eliot goes on to say, despite his initial distaste:

We must be very tolerant of any attempt in verse that appears to trespass upon prose, or of any attempt in prose that appears to strive toward the condition of "poetry." And there is no reason why prose should be confined to any of the recognized forms, the Novel, the Essay, or whatever else there may be in English.

But what exactly does it mean to say that a piece of prose can "strive toward the condition of 'poetry'"? In his introduction to *The Prose Poem*, Michael Benedikt defines the form as "poetry self-consciously written in prose, and characterized by the intense use of virtually all the devices of poetry."[27] On the other hand, as Louis Aragon famously argued, there are no criteria by which to tell a prose poem apart from an "isolated" piece of prose—that is, a brief piece of writing torn from its larger context. Such a text, as Michael Riffaterre suggests, resembles a poem "for the same reason that an object put into a frame or set up on a pedestal becomes a ready-made."[28] With a short piece of prose, one effect of its brevity is to imply, by the white space before and after, that it's somehow special. Hence some short texts will indeed look like prose poems—that is, like works of art to be read and interpreted in reference to other works of art. But some others will look like what they still are, office memos or pieces of a Ross Macdonald novel, or excerpts from a tourist website for Marietta, Ohio. In each instance, the reader is taking cues from the text to determine where it belongs in the universe of literature. A poem, that is, must somehow suggest that it should be read *as a poem.*

According to the transactional theory of literary interpretation, as developed by Louise Rosenblatt, a poem can be seen as an "event," constructed by the relationship (or transaction) between reader and text, just as a team of actors and director and stage crew construct a performance from a script.

> The poem, then, must be thought of as an event in time. It is not an object or an ideal entity. It happens during a coming-together, a compenetration, of a reader and a text. The reader brings to the text his past experience and present personality. Under the magnetism of the ordered symbols of the text, he marshals his resources and crystallizes out from the stuff of memory, thought, and feeling a new order, a new experience, which he sees as the poem.[29]

Furthermore, the reader is responding to the words of the poem or story in the context of his or her knowledge of the entire literary tradition. As Jonathan Culler summarizes, a poem is written—and we might say *read*—"in relation to other poems":

> The communicative intention presupposes listeners who know the language. And similarly, a poem presupposes conventions of reading which the author may work against, which he can transform, but which are the conditions of possibility of his discourse.[30]

At work here are all the expectations a reader brings to the page, expectations of how "a poem" or "a story" will reveal itself, expectations established by various experiences with different sorts of writing. These expectations come to form the framework of the conversation that the reader is having with the text. In Gestalt terms, they are the *ground* upon which the reader sees the *figure* of the piece itself.

When a reader sits down with a book that in its title or subtitle announces itself as a book of poems, she expects to read something which contains certain characteristics she's come to associate with poetry. Conversely, seeing such cues or clues in a text will suggest to her that she's reading a poem. The most obvious features of this sort are rhyme and meter. Other features like heightened diction, metaphoric or difficult language (or sometimes great clarity of language), certain subject matter—mutability, for example (Whitman's "night, sleep, death, and the stars")—all these are often associated with a poetic text, with writing beyond the realm of ordinary discourse. Technically, linguists call this *contextual implicature*; that is, the notion that every speech-act suggests a context within which it will most often be found. A simple example of this is the use of *tu* or *vous* in French conversation, each of which implies a different sort of relationship.

Lineation traditionally serves as a visual cue by which a text presents itself as poetry. As Ruth Finnegan says in her study of the oral poetic tradition, "poetry is normally *typographically* defined."[31] But a person listening to a performance of spoken-word art lacks that cue. Unless the speaker pauses at the end of each line (or unless rhyme and meter are involved), the line-endings disappear in a performance, just as they do in a piece of writing which is typographically prose. In this case a listener or a reader is "forced to look for other, apparently more 'intrinsic' characteristics by which something can be delineated as 'poetry'. . . . not one absolute criterion but a range of stylistic and formal attributes." As Finnegan concludes, "the concept of 'poetry' turns out to be a relative one, depending on a combination of stylistic elements no one of which need necessarily and invariably be present." This sort of definition—one that depends on a preponderance of characteristics—has been used to distinguish categories in anthropology (kinship relations) and biology (taxonomy). In these disciplines it is called *polythetic* classification. The crucial point here is that no single item is necessary, or sufficient, for an item to be recognized as belonging to one category or another—but there must be a critical mass for such recognition to occur.[32] How we interpret any piece of writing depends on the presence or absence of many features, which determine in their totality whether we read the piece as a story, essay, or travel brochure. Or as a poem. We may not be able to make an exhaustive list of such poetic markers, but the impossibility of defining the entire panoply of such characteristics shouldn't blind us to their existence.

In this way the reader determines what kind of language game she is playing with a text—or indeed, what sort of language game the text is playing with her.

And How Does the (Prose) Poem Differ from (Flash) Fiction?

At the end of the day, what we have in the prose poem is a variety of short texts that span the distance between a fairly seamless, or mimetic, description of reality—and a wildly disjunctive, or metaphoric, concatenation of images and thoughts. To use Baudelaire's terms, a piece of prose can alternate between the *supple* and the *jarring*. On the one hand we have short prose narratives such as Ernest Hemingway's "Chapters" from *In Our Time,* and on the other we have pieces like Gertrude Stein's "Objects" in *Tender Buttons.* In the former we see the language of everyday prose, of newspaper articles, of popular novels—with language so transparent that at its best it seems a diaphanous window through which, as a flash of lightning illuminates a landscape, the moment is frozen, caught for an instant, or forever, in the reader's mind.

At the other end of the spectrum we have pieces with what Ron Silliman calls the "new sentence," where the syntax, to use his word, is *torqued,* where there are discontinuities rather than a seamless disquisition—syntax that starts "to go in one direction, only to veer off at unpredictable angles, creating . . . something of far greater power than referential or abstract meaning would lead one to suspect."[33] In my opinion *Tender Buttons* forms the foundation upon which the Language poets and their cohort have established their many-layered structures. Because in this case, as Silliman notes, "it's not about building transparent (or even elegant) grammatical architecture, the transparent prose of a Twain or Bellow, but of representing the shape of time and of experience." This sort of text is metaphoric in the broadest sense of the word, and according to Paul Ricoeur, it "not only shatters the previous structures of our language, but also the previous structures of what we call reality."[34]

It's interesting to compare this kind of writing to what

Bronislaw Malinowski says of the practice of magic among the Trobriand Islanders:

> Magic is not built up in the narrative style; it does not serve to communicate ideas from one person to another; it does not purport to contain a consecutive, consistent meaning. . . . It will not be therefore a meaning of logically or topically concatenated ideas, but of expressions fitting into one another and into the whole, according to what could be called a magical order of thinking, or perhaps more correctly, a magical order of expressing, of launching words towards their aim. It is clear that this magical order of verbal concatenations— I am purposely avoiding the expression "magical logic" for there is no logic in the case—must be known and familiar to anyone who wishes really to understand the spells. There is therefore a great initial difficulty in "reading" such documents, and only an acquaintance with a great number makes one more confident and more competent.[35]

One could substitute *poetry* here for *magic*—or some poetry, anyway—and the paragraph would still make a lot of sense.

The short prose piece can be found anywhere along this continuum, from the magical to the minimal, and at the far end of what we could call the mimetic persuasion we find work like that by Hemingway or Steve Almond, presented in plainspoken language with a strong narrative voice and few linguistic "extras." Will such writing have enough characteristics to flash the light in a given reader's mind that indicates *poem?* Perhaps not. Perhaps its most distinguishing poetic feature is its very brevity, the fact that a page or two of text is all there is, framed by the white space, or silence, surrounding it. At the same time it may have narrative features— dialogue, for example, or other characteristics of tone or point of view—that will suggest to the reader that it be read as fiction, albeit very brief fiction: what Carol Bergé, in 1981, called a "one-page novel."[36]

In an early version of these remarks, I summarized by saying that the dominant type of American prose poem at that time was the one "made so popular by Edson, Benedikt, Ignatow, Merwin, and others: the strange little fantasy." And I went on to suggest that the future might hold a viable alternative, "a more narrative form . . . nearly indistinguishable from a piece of one-page fiction."[37] The emergence of flash fiction as an increasingly popular literary form would seem to bear this out, though of course not all flash fiction would fulfill my definition of poetry. But I'm suggesting that the intersection of the two categories is much larger than the names would suggest; one reader's narrative-prose-poem is another's very-short-story. Russell Edson's little fables, for example, can be found in anthologies of both prose poetry and flash fiction.

Many poems are fictional, but that doesn't make them fiction in the sense that term is generally used. In the common understanding, a piece of fiction must have a plot, though in flash fiction the plot might be implied or presumed—hinted at through the more-or-less transparent window of the prose. As Robert Olen Butler states the case, a piece of flash fiction "is a short short story and not a prose poem because it has at its center a character who yearns." He goes on to say that this yearning is revealed in the telling of the story, and he sums up:

> It has been traditional to think that a story has to have a "plot" while a poem does not. Plot, in fact, is yearning challenged and thwarted. A short short story, in its brevity, may not have a fully developed plot, but it must have the essence of a plot, yearning.[38]

I am indebted for this succinct definition of a story, but I wonder at the implied limitation to the poem. Altogether too many poems, it seems to me, have yearning as their subtext. On the other hand, a quality of interpersonal tension—which often involves yearning—is indeed, at least for this reader, associated with flash fiction. Plot in a "normal" piece of fiction—story, novel, film—involves the working-through of this tension over time. In a piece of flash fiction, the resolution can only be hinted at: the process caught in a single frame, contained in one precise moment.

On the one hand, a traditional narrative is built up by slow degrees, painstakingly over time, layer by layer of impressions like an Old Masters oil painting; on the other hand, flash fiction is like Zen calligraphy, all the creative energy stored like water behind a dam—or electricity in a Leiden jar—released in one burst of activity, lines on paper, the sense of the thing captured in just a few quick strokes. There are works of verse that operate this same way, but we conceive of them as poems rather than stories. Take, for example, Shakespeare's sonnets, which interweave the Narrator, his

Beloved, and the mysterious Other Man. If written in prose, these could make a flash sequence—each individual piece capturing a single emotional configuration—but as it's written in sonnets we focus less on the implied or hidden "plot" and more on the writing itself, each piece shining with what Walter Pater, in another context, called a hard, gem-like flame.

A plot means simply that something *happens* within a story, while in a poem all we can say for sure is that something *is happening*. In fact this is only a question of emphasis. The novel, or story, concerns itself with what physicists call the *arrow of time*, or the arc which any particular arrow follows, while the poem, or lyric, concerns itself with what Buddhists might call the *suchness* of time, the way that things manifest in the moment. Often a piece of writing will do both, and it's a toss-up as to which is predominant—but to the reader, emphasis can often be seen as essence, what the text in question is really "about."

So what's the difference between a prose poem and a piece of flash fiction? I think the question itself reveals a misapprehension. Like the legendary blind men examining an elephant, each one of us feels the particular part of the body he's holding, and no one agrees with the others as to what sort of creature it is that they're touching. Like different tribes with different sorts of kinship relations, we argue over what to call the child who's the son or daughter of a mixed marriage. It's the same kid we're talking about—and let's not forget that. The very question—*What distinguishes a prose poem from a flash?*—presupposes a duality or opposition, a *this-or-that* relationship in which there exists a certain boundary between the two forms. But in fact many pieces of short prose can be conceived as falling into both categories, and in those cases, at least, this is a distinction without a difference. They are two sides of a single coin.

Each reader, I'm suggesting, is responsible for accounting for a particular piece of writing in his or her own way. In transactional terms, you could say that while one reader constructs a poem from a particular text, a different reader may construct a story from the same piece of writing; the act of reading thus defines the text. In its essence the short prose piece, by whatever name, is a hybrid form, located at the crossroads of story and poem. On the one hand we can trace its lineage back through the universe of poetry—rhymed verse, blank verse, free verse—and on the other hand its background includes the whole world of prose—fiction, nonfiction, memos and letters home. Those who call what they write *flash fiction* see themselves as heirs of a whole tradition of storytellers, and those who write *prose poems* see themselves in a long line of poets. The reality, of course, is that poets are, many of them, storytellers—just as storytellers, many of them, are poets. Both schools have ended up being drawn to the same classroom, short prose, but each sees that *short* as a different sort of place.

The story, whatever name it takes, has as part of its charm that it's written in what we can call the language of the quotidian, language that purports to tell of the real world. Poetry, on the other hand, by its very nature exists beyond the realm of ordinary discourse—and this combination of opposites is what makes the prose poem so endlessly fascinating. While prose rises organically from the everyday, poetry with its long tradition of "nightingales and psalms" has about it something transcendent—something, we might say, of the sacred. In this way the prose poem, child of two worlds, serves to bring together, at long last, the sacred and mundane.

—Robert Alexander

1. Shapiro 1975, 342–343.
2. Spackman 1975, 189–190
3. "Now that the prose poem is a dominant American iterary form, we call Edson a prose poet, but he is doing precisely the same 'Fables'—short stories of extraordinary fantasy and caprice—that he was doing in 1964 . . ." (Hall 1977, 12).
4. Quoted in Flanner 1975, xiv.
5. Anderson 1942, 246

6. Boyle 1967, 11.
7. Quoted in Wagner 1970, 8.
8. Edson 1980, 300.
9. See, for example, Thompson 1977.
10. Hunt 2003, 146–153.
11. Baudelaire 196, 6–7; translated by the author, who is indebted to Raymond Mackenzie for the use of "jarring" for *heurtée*.
12. "*Style.—La note éternel et cosmopolite. Chateaubriand, Alph. Rabbe, Edgar Poe.*" (Quoted in Moreau 1959, 26.)
13. Glicksberg 1933, 17; Whitman's pen name for these articles was Velsor Brush.
14. Hearn 1919, 147-151; also Alexander 1996, 20-22.
15. Merrill 1890, v, vii.
16. Williams 1957, 6.
17. Boyle 1936, xii-xiii.
18. Masih 2009, xxiv.
19. Eliot 1957, 109.
20. Poe 1914, 6: 34-35.
21. Almond 2009, 107-108.
22. Chaytor 1966, 83, 85.
23. Rutsala 1978, 18.
24. Young 1977.
25. For a more thorough treatment of heteroglossia (and of the American prose poem in general) see Murphy 1992.

26. Eliot 1921, 3-9, 10.

27. Benedikt 1976, 47.

28. Riffaterre 1978, 116.
29. Rosenblatt 1994, 12.
30. Culler 1975, 30.
31. Finnegan 1977, 25.
32. "No feature is essential for membership in a polythetically defined taxon nor is any feature sufficient for such membership" (Mayr 1969, 83).
33. Silliman 2007.

34. Ricoeur 1978, 132.
35. Malinowski 1978, 338-39.
36. Bergé 1981.
37. Alexander 1982, 56.
38. Butler 2009, 102-103.

CONTRIBUTORS' NOTES

Virginia Admiral (1915–2000)

These days, Virginia Admiral is perhaps primarily remembered as the mother of the actor Robert De Niro, Jr., though she had a long career as a visual artist. As the *New York Times* reported in her obituary:

> Ms. Admiral was born in Oregon and studied at the Art Institute of Chicago. . . . in 1938, she became closely involved with the San Francisco poetry scene. With the poet Robert Duncan she published a single issue of a small-press magazine, *Epitaph*, which developed into the *Experimental Review*. . . . In 1940 she enrolled at the Hofmann School in New York to study painting. . . . In 1942 Ms. Admiral exhibited in the Springs Salon for Young Artists at at Peggy Guggenheim's Art of This Century Gallery in Manhattan. She had a solo show there in 1946 and was included in the Peggy Guggenheim Collection at the Venice Biennale in 1947. In the 1960's Ms. Admiral was active in the antiwar movement. . . . Her work is in the permanent collections of the Metropolitan Museum of Art, the Museum of Modern Art in New York and the Peggy Guggenheim Collection in Venice. (15 August 2000)

"The Escaped Bear" was published in the *Experimental Review* (January 1941) and has not been reprinted since.

Margaret C. Anderson (1886–1973)

From the perspective of the American prose poem, the founding of *The Little Review,* by Margaret Anderson in March, 1914, is probably among the dozen most important events in the entire history of Modernism. Perhaps I should amend that sentence to read, "from the perspective of American Modernism, the founding of *The Little Review* is among the dozen most important events." Margaret Anderson was, to say the least, an iconic figure in the Chicago Renaissance of the early twentieth century. Later she moved the magazine to New York City (and then Paris) and was involved in the obscenity trial which came about as a result of her publication, in serial form, of James Joyce's *Ulysses.* (The prosecutor refused to read the offending passages aloud as he was in the presence of a young beautiful woman—that is to say, Ms. Anderson herself, the publisher of the very piece he took exception to.)

Harry Hansen quotes an unnamed individual in his *Midwest Portraits:*

> She was always exquisite, as if emerging from a scented boudoir, not from a mildewed tent or a camp where frying bacon was scenting the atmosphere. She was always vivid, is yet, and beautiful to look upon . . . her fluffy hair blows marvelously, her eyes are in Lake Michigan's best blue. (Hansen 1923, 105)

But perhaps the most revealing story about her comes from the pen of Emma Goldman:

> During my stay [in Chicago] I came upon the new liter-

ary publication called *The Little Review,* and shortly afterwards I met its editor, Margaret C. Anderson. I felt like a desert wanderer who unexpectedly discovers a stream of fresh water. At last a magazine to sound a note of rebellion in creative endeavor! . . .

In a large apartment facing Lake Michigan I found, besides Miss Anderson . . . a girl named Harriet Dean. The entire furniture consisted of a piano, piano-stool, several broken cots, a table, and some kitchen chairs. . . .

Harriet Dean was as much a novel type to me as Margaret, yet the two were entirely unlike. Harriet was athletic, masculine-looking, reserved, and self-conscious. Margaret, on the contrary, was feminine in the extreme, constantly bubbling over with enthusiasm. A few hours with her entirely changed my first impression and made me realize that underneath her apparent lightness was depth and strength of character to pursue whatever aim in life she might choose. (Goldman 1934, 530–31)

Two of the pieces attributed to Anderson in this anthology represent something of a mystery. "Ocean Acquarium" and "Landscape" have not traditionally been attributed to Anderson. In the table of contents for the issue of *The Little Review* in which they appeared (*LR* 9, No. 3, Autumn 1922), these pieces are in fact unattributed, a practice not uncommon for Ms. Anderson's own editorial comments. On the cover, this issue is titled "Stella Number," and it includes, as the table of contents indicates, "16 Reproductions of the work of Joseph Stella." The two pieces in

Autumn   1922

THE LITTLE REVIEW

QUARTERLY JOURNAL
OF ART AND LETTERS

SUBSCRIPTION

YEARLY: $4.00   £1 FOREIGN

SINGLE NUMBER
$1.00

ADMINISTRATION

Margaret ANDERSON   jh   **Ezra POUND**
Francis PICABIA

address: 27 west eighth street, new york
english office: egoist publishing co., 23 adelphi
terrace house, robert street, london w. c. 2.

Entered as second class matter october 28, 1921, at the post office at new york, n. y., under the act of march 2, 1879.

CONTENTS

ON SALE ALL FIRST CLASS BOOK STORES
F. B. NEUMAYER: 70 CHARING CROSS ROAD LONDON
SHAKESPEARE AND COMPANY: PARIS VIe
VOL. IX   NO. 1

question are found, in the table of contents, just before and after this listing, and all three items are blank in the column which lists contributors' names. In the issue itself, the two prose pieces are to be found on consecutive pages, just before a spread of four Stella images. The piece that preceeds them is by Isidor Schneider, and hence it appears that these two paragraphs should perhaps also be attributed to him. However, Schneider tended to concern himself in his poetry with other things, as this comment from the introduction to *Comrade: Mister* (1934) would indicate: "The period of revolutionary struggle is upon us. . . . and the poets look to it for new subject matter." Schneider's non-political poetry, such as it is, reveals qualities very different from these two prose pieces— though they are, in my opinion, stylistically quite similar to Anderson's own writing in *My Thirty Years War* (1930).

Apparently Margaret Anderson was sometimes loath to put her name in a table of contents: another piece of hers, "Imagism," is included in *The Little Review Anthology* (1953), which she edited, but neither poem nor author is listed in that book's table of contents. This piece was excerpted by Anderson herself from "The Piano and Imagism," originally published in August 1915, and consists, as she wrote in a contemporary footnote, of phrases "taken from the Imagists." For the later version that appears here, Anderson entirely cut the first paragraph of the original. "Toward Revolution" was a signed editorial that same year in *The Little Review* (December 1915), and shows a political dimension which occasionally surfaced in the magazine. As she relates in *My Thirty Years War*, she lost the support of a substantial funder because of a laudatory piece she wrote about Emma Goldman.

Sherwood Anderson (1876–1941)

A businessman from Ohio who in his late thirties ran away from home to become a writer in Chicago, Sherwood Anderson was one of the loosely-knit group that helped create what he called "a robin's-egg Renaissance" (so named, as he said, because "it fell out of the nest"). The author of many books, he is perhaps best known for his short story collection, *Winesburg, Ohio* (1919), which showcases his mastery of characterization and place as well as his penchant for using a plain-spoken voice, the same voice that he had earlier used in *Mid-American Chants* (1918). *The Little Review Anthology* starts off with a piece by Sherwood Anderson from the first issue of *The Little Review* (March 1914), titled, "The New Note":

> The new note in the craft of writing is in danger, as are all new and beautiful things born into the world, of being talked to death. . . . In the trade of writing the so-called new note is as old as the world. Simply stated, it is a cry for the reinjection of truth and honesty into the craft; it is an appeal from the standards set up by money-making magazine and book publishers in Europe and America to the older, sweeter standards of the craft itself. . . .
>
> It is the most delicate and unbelievably difficult task to catch, understand, and record your own mood. The thing must be done simply and without pretense or windiness, for the moment these creep in your record is no longer a record, but a mere mass of words meaning nothing. (Anderson 1953, 13–14)

In my opinion, it makes sense to call Anderson the first modern "Midwest" prose poet, a loose stylistic grouping that would later include James Wright and Robert Bly. In Anderson, moreover, it's possible to see the confluence of two movements, one toward an American diction, the other toward literary experiments such as the prose poem. In this regard he's like William Carlos Williams.

Two of the poems included here, "The Cornfields" and "Song of the Soul of Chicago," were first published in the "Chicago Number" of *Others* (June 1917), and were later included in *Mid-American Chants*. "Sister" first appeared in *The Little Review* (December 1915), and has been reprinted in Anderson's *Early Writings* (1989). "The Lame One" first appears as the creation of a character in the novel *Dark Laughter* (1925, 121–122), and was then included in the anthology *Lyric America* (1930), edited by Alfred Kreymborg, the brilliant editor of *Others*. The version that appears in *Dark Laughter* has the dedication, "To J. J."—an indication of just how long a shadow was cast by James Joyce.

Holly Beye (1922–2011)

Holly Beye grew up in Iowa, and after graduating from Swarthmore in 1943 she went to New York city to pursue a career as a writer. In 1946 she married the artist David Ruff. Their life together as struggling artists in Greenwich Village in the late forties was recounted in her journal, only recently published: *120 Charles Street, The Village* (2006). It was at this time that Beye became a friend and student of Kenneth Patchen, who was then living in Connecticut. In fact, it was Patchen who suggested that Beye keep a journal, and it was at this time that Beye began to experiment with the prose poem. In 1951, tired of living in poverty in a depressingly urban environment, she and her husband moved to San Francisco, where they became part of the early Beat community. Her books of prose poems were published there. Later she and her husband moved to Woodstock, NY, where they divorced, and Beye began writing plays, a literary form more to her liking as a social activist. She died in January 2011, shortly after sending me permission to include her work in this anthology. (Her obituary appears in the *Woodstock Daily Freeman*, 9 January 2011.)

Two of the poems here are taken from *In the City of Sorrowing Clouds* (1953): "For the Singer That Is Gone" and "In the Eucalyptus Forest." Four poems are taken from *Stairwells & Marriages* (1955b): "Faces in a Furious Night," "The Unremitting Stain," "The Release of Hostages," and "Some New Notches with an Old Knife."

In 1955, Kenneth Patchen had this to say: "For some years it has been my conviction that Holly Beye is one of the most gifted of the young American writers" (Beye 1955a, front flyleaf).

Paul Bowles (1910–1999)

Paul Bowles was raised in New York City and attended the University of Virginia. Equally talented and productive as both a writer and composer, he is probably best remembered these days as the author of *The Sheltering Sky*, a melancholy novel, originally published in 1949, which was made into a movie in 1990 by Bernardo Bertolucci (starring Debra Winger and John Malkovich). In the late forties Paul Bowles and his wife Jane Auer Bowles settled in Tangier, where Gertrude Stein had first suggested he visit, and where they lived, sometimes separately, for the rest of their lives (she died in 1973), though they both continued to travel widely. During the era of the Beats and thereafter, the two of them became iconic figures, and many writers made a pilgrimage to the Bowles' home in North Africa. His ashes are buried in upstate New York.

Bowles' work here is excerpted from "No Village," a sequence in eight parts taken from *The Thicket of Spring* (1972). There is a note at the end of this sequence dating it to 1930.

Kay Boyle (1902–1992)

One of the most prolific writers of a prolific generation, Kay Boyle published two dozen works of fiction, half a dozen books of poetry, and several collections of nonfiction. She grew up in St. Paul, Minnesota, and spent several decades abroad, including a stint as foreign correspondent for the *New Yorker*. Returning to America in the sixties, she taught for nearly twenty years at San Francisco State University.

"Summer" appeared in 1925 in the first issue of *This Quarter*, a magazine edited by Ernest Walsh, a poet with whom Boyle conceived a child, and who died at the age of thirty-one from tuberculosis. These pieces have never been collected, so far as I know, and are not included in Boyle's *Collected Poems* (1962). The two pieces titled "January 1" and "January 24" appeared in *365 Days* (1936), which was edited by Boyle, her then-husband Laurence Vail, and Nina Conarain, later the author of thirty-two Harlequin romance novels under the pseudonym Elizabeth Hoy. "January 24" was reprinted in the first issue of *New Directions* (1936). Boyle's "For an American," a multi-part poem mixing prose and free verse, of which I've included the first two parts, was dated 1926 (written after Walsh's death in October of that year) and was published in her first book of poetry, *A Glad Day* (1938).

Emily Holmes Coleman (1899–1974)

Emily Holmes was born in Oakland, California, and graduated from Wellesley College in 1920. In 1921 she married the psychologist Lloyd Ring Coleman. She moved to Paris in 1926 and worked for the European edition of the *Chicago Tribune.* For a year she assisted Emma Goldman in the writing of her autobiography, *Living My Life* (1934), and continued to live in Europe in the 1930s and '40s. She had a wide circle of literary friends, included among whom were Djuna Barnes, Edwin Muir, and Peggy Guggenheim. In 1944 she converted to Catholicism and became a supporter of Dorothy Day. She is buried in Tivoli, NY.

Though a prolific writer, her only published work includes stories in little magazines and a single novel, *The Shutter of Snow* (1930), based in part on her own experience of postpartum depression. A second novel remains unpublished. As Joseph Gerci wrote in her obituary:

> She was intense and passionate, sometimes to the point of mania. She was remarkable, reasonable, and quite simply the most important influence on the lives of those who knew her. (Rood 1980, 72)

"The Wren's Nest" first appeared in *transition*'s "American Number" (Summer 1928) and was included in *Transition Stories*

(1929), and later in the anthology *Transition Workshop* (1949). It is an example of the short prose sequence in which the component parts are interrelated and tightly woven, one of several that can be found in this anthology.

Harry Crosby (1898–1929)

On December 10, 1929, Harry Crosby, 31, and Josephine Rotch Bigelow, 22, were found dead together in a friend's apartment. They'd been lovers for a year and a half, though each was married to someone else. It was ruled a double suicide. In the minds of many people, this was a symbolic end to the 1920s, following as it did the stock market crash of October. It was a tragic loss. Crosby, the nephew by marriage of J. P. Morgan, was not only a poet but also a wealthy supporter of the literary community. He and his wife Caresse founded Black Sun Books in Paris, which published, among other important books, the first edition of Hart Crane's self-styled "epic of the modern consciousness," *The Bridge*.

On the boat from France to America in 1929, Crosby copied in longhand the prose poems included in *Sleeping Together*, intended as a gift for Caresse. A few days later he was dead. In June 1930, *transition* published excerpts from *Sleeping Together*, along with remembrances by some of his friends. The following passage is taken from Kay Boyle's tribute:

> There was no one who ever lived more consistently in the thing that was happening then. And with that courage to meet whatever he had chosen, with no consistency except the consistency of his own choice, and

always the courage to match it. His heart was like an open door, so open that there was a crowd getting into it. (Boyle 1930, 222)

The poems I've included here are taken from a complete reprinting of the book in *American Caravan 4* (1931), as copies of the book itself are extremely rare. It is, in my opinion, high time that someone bring out another edition of this important work.

E. E. Cummings (1894–1962)

As a Modernist poet, Cummings is too well-known to need an introduction. In his books published during the 1920s he included occasional prose poems, two of which can be found here. His contribution, in my opinion, as far as the prose poem is concerned at any rate, is that he loosened things up and began to create a context in which poets could take playful chances. Different as their work is, it's perhaps not too much of a stretch to say that if it weren't for Cummings, Kenneth Patchen—and later, Russell Edson—might not have graced us with their priceless little constructions.

"i was sitting in mcsorley's" is one of the thirteen sections of "Post Impressions"—four of which are prose—and was first published in *&* (1925); "at the ferocious phenomenon of 5 o'clock" is from "Portraits"—which includes nine pieces, two of which are prose—also published in 1925 in *XLI Poems.* Both pieces are included in Cummings' *Complete Poems* (1962).

Harriet Dean (1892–1964)

Harriet Dean was, for a time, Margaret Anderson's partner and the business manager of *The Little Review.* We have already seen, in Margaret Anderson's notes (above), the comment that Emma Goldman made about Dean, and we also have a record of her later sojourn in California from the artist Elsie Whitaker Martinez. The following remarks have been excerpted from an oral interview with Martinez conducted in 1969:

> [Harriet Dean's] mother was a Daughter of the American Revolution from New England. . . . The Silas Dean[e] that went to Europe with Franklin was one of that family. . . . She grew up a rockbound Republican, as her father's family were industrialists in the Middle West. . . .
>
> Harriet was a remarkable pianist; there wasn't anything she couldn't do with a piano. . . . She had a genius for that sort of thing. . . . She was trained to be a pianist—her mother's ambition. . . .
>
> She looked like a businesswoman . . . and was very persuasive. She could go into any office in Chicago and would try to convince them of the cultural importance of *The Little Review* and often the business heads would give her a check for a hundred or a couple hundred dollars. . . .
>
> And then after about two or three years she left *The Little Review.* . . . *The Little Review* became famous and got on its feet. It had a large subscription list and some donors, so they did not need her. But there was no disagreement of any kind. (Martinez 1969, 229–32)

The poems I include by Dean were first published in 1916 in *The Little Review:* "Debutante" in the January–February issue, and "Barn-Yarding" and "Departure" in June–July. Neither has ever been reprinted.

H. D. (1886–1961)

Hilda Doolittle was a college friend of both Ezra Pound and William Carlos Williams at the University of Pennsylvania. A prolific writer, she has eighty-five listings in the Library of Congress Catalog—but no prose poems are included in her *Collected Poems.* Nonetheless, in 1929, right at the brink of the Depression, two prose poems appeared in consecutive issues of the little magazine *Blues: A Magazine of New Rhythms* (June and July), edited by Charles Henri Ford, then a student at the University of Mississippi. According to her statement in the Contributors' Notes, they are part of "a series of Four Prose Choruses," though only two appeared in *Blues.* Like much of H. D's work, these pieces are animated by her great respect for and, indeed, fascination with the Erotic and Ecstatic. But like much of the rest of American experimentation with the prose poem, they have been pretty much ignored and lost to view. The complete four "Prose Choruses," accompanied by a "Prose Corybantic," were printed in their entirety in *Agenda* (1987, 9–23), an issue which includes further bibliographical information—but the versions I'm using are the ones that appeared during her lifetime.

Robert Duncan (1919–1988)

Robert Duncan's career is too complex to be to be summed up

in a sentence or two, but one thing that can be said for certain is that he was doing a lot of experimenting with the prose poem in the 1940s and 1950s. As editor of the *Experimental Review* he also gave space to other prose poets, among them Holly Beye and Mary Fabilli. The pieces by Duncan I've included here combine the opacity and precision that for me characterize so much of his work. Though some of his prose poems are by his own admission derivative of Gertrude Stein, he went on to develop his own hermetic style. I quite agree with Mary Fabilli, who has called Duncan "a magician of the marvelous" (Fabilli 1968, 3). At his best Duncan leaves me gasping for breath, so clean and perfect are his sentences:

> We live within ourselves then, like honest woodsmen
> within a tyrannical forest, a magical element. Sheltered
> by our imaginary humble lives from the eternal storm
> of our rage. ("Unkingd by Affection")

"At Home," "Correspondences," and "Source" are taken from *Letters* (1958). "Unkingd by Affection" was originally included in a group of poems sent to friends for Christmas, 1952, and later was published in *Writing, writing* (1964). "Concerning the Maze" first appeared in the *Experimental Review* (September 1941), and is included in *Derivations* (1968).

T. S. Eliot (1888–1965)

In 1917, the same year that William Carlos Williams' "The Delicacies" appeared in *The Egoist*, T. S. Eliot published *Prufrock*, a book which contains "Hysteria," the only prose poem he published in his lifetime, and which had first appeared in 1915 in Ezra Pound's *Catholic Anthology*. I am using here the version that appears in Eliot's *Complete Poems and Plays* (1962). The other piece by Eliot that I include, "The Engine," didn't see the light of day until the publication of *Inventions of the March Hare*, in 1996. According to Margueritte Murphy, there are at least two other prose poems among Eliot's manuscripts in the Berg Collection of the New York Public Library. These pieces taken together reveal some of Eliot's preoccupations with the poet adrift in modern society, disoriented by the more overt eroticism of the "new woman." Unfortunately, as Murphy says,

> Given Eliot's stature and influence over his generation
> of poets and critics, and over subsequent generations of
> professors of English, I wonder . . . whether his lack of
> sustained interest in the prose poem, as well as Ezra
> Pound's, helped keep the form at the margins of mod-
> ernist poetry in English. (Murphy 1992; 52, 211 n. 87,
> 59–60)

Mary Fabilli (1914–2011)

Mary Fabilli was born in New Mexico, where her parents, Italian immigrants, had come to work in Gardiner, a mining town. They moved often while she was growing up, and she graduated from high school in California and entered UC-Berkeley, graduating in 1941. During the war, she worked at the Kaiser shipyard in Richmond, then spent most of her career working at the Oakland Museum. She was married to William Everson, whom she met in

1946, until their marriage was annulled when he joined the Dominican Friars. More information about her can be found in Brenda Knight's *Women of the Beat Generation.*

In Fabilli's own words:

> The Aurora Bligh stories were written in the late 1930's and the 40's in Berkeley, California—for a small audience consisting of Robert Duncan, Virginia Admiral, my sister Lili, and a few others. It did not occur to me that complete strangers might find them either entertaining or intelligible. . . .
>
> When spring comes around each year in Berkeley and the Japanese plum trees bloom and February winds scatter their petals through the air I am reminded of the excitement of those early friendships, our feverish dedication to the arts, our quarrels, criticisms and misunderstandings, the reconciliations, the sharing of plans, inspirations, rebellions; and the constant anxiety caused by lack of financial resources and the scarcity of part-time jobs. (Fabilli 1968, 3)

As poems of alienation, moving or attempting to move toward redemption with a restrained and rather grim surrealism, Fabilli's work can be seen as indicative of a strong link between the prose poetry of the twenties and that of a later generation. The innovations of the fifties didn't birth themselves, in other words—but in fact owe a lot to an earlier period of experimentation. "The Morning Led" and "This Is the Day of Freedom" were first published in 1941 in the *Experimental Review*, and later appeared in *Aurora Bligh & Early Poems* (1968), as did "They in Whose Dreams" and "Poem." Mary Fabilli died in September 2011, while I was completing the final draft of this anthology. She lived long enough to give me permission to reprint her work, for which I am very grateful.

William Faulkner (1897–1962)

As a young man, residing for a time in New Orleans, William Faulkner made a stab at newspaper writing. His work appeared in the Sunday supplement of the *Times-Picayune*. He also submitted poetry and sketches—such as the ones included here—to the *Double Dealer*, before turning his hand to the fiction that would later win him the Nobel Prize for literature. Published in New Orleans, *The Double Dealer*, as we'll later see with Jean Toomer and Thornton Wilder, is another example of how specific editors of little magazines, in this case John McClure, were of great importance to the history of American poetry—and American prose poetry in particular. The pieces included here are all included in *New Orleans Sketches* (1958). More specifically, they are taken from "New Orleans," which was originally published in the *Double Dealer* (January–February 1925).

John Gould Fletcher (1886–1950)

Born and raised in Little Rock, Arkansas, Fletcher like many upperclass young men from the South attended school in Massachusetts: first, Phillips Andover Academy and then, Harvard. After his father died, leaving Fletcher a substantial sum of money, Fletcher dropped out of college and went to England, where he stayed until 1933. There he fell in with Ezra Pound and other Modernists, and became associated with the *Egoist* magazine. It was Pound who introduced him to Amy Lowell, and Pound who sent his poems to Harriet Monroe at *Poetry* magazine. Fletcher became known as an Imagist, appearing in Lowell's 1915 anthology, *Some Imagist Poets.*

After returning to America during the Depression, Fletcher became a member of the Southern Agrarians, who were proponents of a less industrial, and in many ways more traditional, way of life. See, for example, Fletcher's essay, "Education, Past and Present," in the anthology, *I'll Take My Stand* (1930). Tragically, suffering from severe depression, Fletcher drowned himself in 1950. The first three pieces included here first appeared with several others in *Broom*, a little magazine with a large subtitle: *An International Magazine of the Arts published by Americans in Italy* (January 1922), and were reprinted, along with "The End of Job," in *Parables* (1925).

Charles Henri Ford (1908–2002)

Charles Henri Ford's most important single contribution to the world of the prose poem might well have been his "Little Anthology of the Poem in Prose," published in *New Directions* 14 in 1953 (Ford's comment that the prose poem is the form of the future is quoted by Parker Tyler in the preface). But such a statement undercuts the vast influence Ford had on both Modernism and Postmodernism, as a writer, editor, and friend. Raised in Brookhaven, Mississippi, Ford dropped out of high school to attend the University of Mississippi, where he published his first magazine, *Blues: A Magazine of New Rhythms*, while still an undergraduate. After that he moved to Paris and became acquainted with Gertrude Stein, Kay Boyle, Man Ray, Peggy Guggenheim, Djuna Barnes, to name just a few members of the expatriate community whom Ford knew. At the suggestion of Paul Bowles, he traveled to Morocco—and while there, according to his obituary, he typed up Djuna Barnes' *Nightwood,* which she'd just completed (http://www.milkmag.org/fordpage.htm). In 1933 he published *The Young and the Evil* with Parker Tyler, a novel which was banned in France as well as in America.

Returning to New York in 1934, accompanied by his partner Pavel Tchelitchew, Ford started associating (again according to his obituary) with folks such as Carl Van Vechten, Glenway Wescott, Lincoln Kirstein, Orson Welles, George Balanchine, and E. E. Cummings. The forties magazine *View,* which he published, focused on visual art, accepting work by Max Ernst, Pablo Picasso, Henry Miller, Paul Klee, and Georgia O'Keeffe, among others.

Nor did Ford's career end there. For years he lived in the Dakota apartment building in New York City, and was involved in the many incarnations the New York artistic and literary worlds went through in the twentieth century. As his obituary concludes, "Ford was a revolutionary and provocateur, who led many lives and mastered many various disciplines." "Suite" first appeared in *Blues* (Fall 1929) and has not previously been reprinted. "Flag of Ecstasy" and "Message to Rimbaud" were included in Ford's "Little Anthology of the Poem in Prose," and were both reprinted in *Flag of Ecstasy* (1972).

Jane Heap (1883–1964)

For many years, working and living with Margaret Anderson, Jane Heap co-edited *The Little Review*. Her arrival at the magazine in the spring of 1916 was, according to Anderson, "the most interesting thing that ever happened to the magazine" (Anderson 1930, 63). Heap was born and raised in Topeka, Kansas, where her father was warden of what was then called a "mental asylum." After high school she moved to Chicago, where she studied at the Art Institute and became an instructor at the Lewis Institute. In 1912 she helped found Maurice Browne's Little Theater. In 1916 she met Margaret Anderson and became her partner at *The Little Review*. In the latter days of the magazine, after it had moved to Paris, Heap became the sole editor, until it folded in 1929. Her influence, as well as Anderson's, on the development of modern literature remains, still, a fertile area for research.

"Sketches" first appeared in *The Little Review* (November 1917), and was reprinted in *The Little Review Anthology*, where Margaret Anderson said of it, "Jane Heap wrote her first creative piece . . . which, with its 'zones of pain where one may rest,' still has emotional importance . . ." (Anderson 1953, 148; ellipses in original). "Paris at One Time" was also first published in *The Little Review* and reprinted in *The Little Review Anthology*. As Anderson said of it,

> The last piece of prose in *The Little Review* that compelled my enthusiasm appeared in the summer number of 1926. It was by Jane and I felt that its beautiful and powerful imagery surpassed anything that the Surrealists had done. I still feel so. (Anderson 1953, 344)

Ernest Hemingway (1899–1961)

While living in Paris, Ernest Hemingway took writing lessons from Ezra Pound in exchange for boxing and tennis lessons. One possible result of this collaboration was the prose sequence "in our time." One biographer, Jeffrey Meyers, states that "the first six vignettes of *in our time* were written in January–February 1923" (Meyers 1985, 141). They were first published in 1923 in *The Little Review* "Exiles Number," which though it was titled a spring issue didn't actually didn't appear until the fall of the year—an issue edited by Foreign Editor Ezra Pound. In somewhat different form, along with a dozen additional pieces written slightly later, they were published in 1924 by Bill Bird's Three Mountains Press in a tiny chapbook edition, also titled *in our time*—part of a series edited by Pound as an "inquest into the state of modern English prose" (Cohen 2003, 107). These pieces, with numeric headings, lived on as dividers or "interchapters," as they've been called, between the stories in Hemingway's first collection, which was called, once again, *In Our Time* (1925). I have included here the first five that were published in *The Little Review*, as well as the last, "L'Envoi," the only piece to have a non-numeric title. Hemingway's work here exemplifies the statement he made about his writing, "The secret is that it is poetry written into prose and it is the hardest of all things to do" (Tetlow 1992, 13).

Tara Masih, editor of the Rose Metal *Field Guide to Writing Flash Fiction*, describes the pieces of *in our time* as early examples of short short stories, a precursor of flash fiction (Masih 2009, xii). Moreover, *in our time* is interesting not only because it serves as an historical anchor for flash, but also because it's an early example (in prose, at any rate) of a form we can call the sequence-of-vignettes. In a sense this form is very old indeed, one example being the Elizabethan sonnet sequence. More modern incarnations have a close relationship to cinematic montage.

Fenton Johnson (1888–1958)

Fenton Johnson grew up in Chicago, the son of a railroad porter who was reportedly one of the wealthiest African-Americans in Chicago. He attended Northwestern University, the University of Chicago, and the Columbia University School of Journalism. In 1918 he began publishing the *Favorite Magazine*, which billed itself "the first and only weekly magazine published by and for colored people." In the twenties he founded the Reconciliation Movement, whose mission was to improve relations between blacks and whites. His poems included here were part of a longer manuscript, which has been lost, also entitled "African Nights." Another unpublished manuscript, "The Daily Grind: 41 WPA Poems," can be found in the Fisk University Library Special Collections. For more information about Johnson, see Patton and Honey (2001). "African Nights" first appeared in *Others* (February 1919) and can also be found in *Others for 1919*, both edited by Alfred Kreymborg (1920).

Amy Lowell (1874–1925)

Amy Lowell was born and raised and lived in Brookline, Massachusetts, where she became known as "the bard of Brookline." Physically quite imposing, and often smoking little cigars, she wrote what she called "metrical prose"—which John Gould Fletcher amended to the more mellifluous "polyphonic prose"—the intention of which was to write what was typographically prose but which would use all the traditional devices of verse: rhyme, regularity of rhythm, and even meter when it seemed appropriate (Lowell 1914, 213–20; Fletcher 1915, 32–36). Lowell's idea, in other words, was to use aspects of poeticalness which don't generally find their way into prose poems. As she said, her form is based "upon the long, flowing cadences of oratorical prose," a style which was even then being spurned in favor of a more down-to-earth poetic voice (Lowell 1918, xii). This new "prosey" voice is in fact one of the hallmarks of the Modernist American prose poem, and the tension between traditional and more plainspoken diction is an underlying element in its development. The four pieces here are taken from the sequence, "Spring Day," originally published in *Men, Women and Ghosts* (1917).

Robert McAlmon (1896–1956)

Robert McAlmon grew up partly in South Dakota, a place that would figure significantly in his work, and he enlisted in 1918 in the U.S. Army Air Corps. After the war, he attended college in California and moved to Chicago and then New York. He published *Contact* with William Carlos Williams, a short-lived cheaply-produced journal, and then, as so many Americans did at that time, he moved to Paris to take advantage of the strong dollar. In 1921 he married H. D.'s partner, Bryher, whose name at birth was Winifred Ellerman, the daughter of one of the wealthiest men in England (they divorced in 1927). Above all, her family did not want to be embarrassed socially because their daughter was gay, and McAlmon was happy to spend their money publishing Contact

Editions.

McAlmon's *Being Geniuses Together, 1920–1930* (later published with supplementary material by Kay Boyle), is one of the most interesting chronicles of the era. Several years after the prose poem "Village" was published, McAlmon published a novel by the same name, about life in a bleak mid-American town—though it is not, like the poem, told in first person. Only recently published for the first time, McAlmon's *Nightinghouls of Paris* (2007) is an intriguing roman-à-clef about the decline of the expatriate world of the '20s.

In my opinion, McAlmon's work is significant specifically because of the kind of narrative framework he brings to the form—a framework that has become increasingly important in the intervening years, as is evidenced by the explosive growth of flash fiction. There's a simplicity in McAlmon's writing that Hemingway may have learned from—or vice versa: in fact, McAlmon was the publisher of Hemingway's first book, *Three Stories & Ten Poems* (1923). McAlmon's prose poems are taken from his first book, *Explorations* (1921), one section of which is entitled "Prose Sketches."

Kenneth Patchen (1911–1972)

Kenneth Patchen's work in poetry, prose, and art is too voluminous to categorize or easily catalog. For this reader, Patchen's prose poems are stylistically remarkable for the accuracy of his voice and his ability to switch registers so quickly. Though he lived for a time in San Francisco, and was in retrospect an important figure in the San Francisco Renaissance of the 1950s, he disavowed any connection with the Beats. As he said in the "Statement" on the back cover of *Poemscapes*, a collection of very short prose poems published in 1958, "my participation in, and knowledge of, 'the San Francisco Scene,' are exactly zero. My stay there was occasioned and colored by medical considerations; unfortunately those of a social or literary kind did not enter into it."

Despite this disavowal, Patchen's performances that combined poetry and jazz accompaniment were seminal to the development of this phenomenon in the Beat and post-Beat world. As Kenneth Rexroth wrote at the end of the fifties, "against a conspiracy of silence of the whole of literary America, Patchen has become the laureate of the doomed youth of the Third World War. He is the most widely read younger poet in the country" (Rexroth 1959, 100).

"Polly—An Almost-True Story" was first published in *The Teeth of the Lion* (1942); "Family Portrait" first appeared in *Red Wine & Yellow Hair* (1949); and "O What a Revolution!" and "There Are Two" are taken from *The Famous Boating Party and other poems in prose* (1954), which contains fifty-four pieces, none of which had ever been published before. These poems were all published in final form in *When We Were Here Together: Collected Poems* (1957).

"A Pasturized Scene" is from a unique little book, *Fables & Other Little Tales* (1953)—which according to an introductory essay by Jonathan Williams, was written in 1950. This, incidentally, is the same time period during which Patchen was working with Holly Beye on her prose poems. *Fables* was reprinted by New Directions as *Aflame and Afun of Walking Faces* (1970); of all the books I can think of, it can only be compared, favorably, with Carl Sandburg's *Rootabaga Stories*, which was published in 1922, and which perhaps Patchen was familiar with as a youngster.

Laura Riding [Jackson] (1901–1991)

Laura Reichenthal was born in New York City and educated at Cornell University. She began publishing poetry, notably in the *Fugitive* magazine, as Laura Riding Gottshalk. After divorcing Louis Gottschalk in 1925, she went overseas along with much of literary America, having been invited to England by Robert Graves and his wife Nancy Nicholson. This situation ended badly in 1929, after which Riding and Graves moved to Majorca and collaborated on the Seizin Press, a small literary imprint. At the outbreak of the Spanish Civil War in 1936, Riding and Graves left Majorca and a few years later they parted ways. In 1941 she married Schuyler B. Jackson, and in the early forties she renounced the practice of poetry, "as disappointing the hopes it excites as seemingly the way of perfect human utterance, or articulate truth" (Jackson 2007, 29).

For some readers, Riding's work will seem out of place in an anthology of the prose poem—and that in itself illustrates the subjective limits of the form. Her work inhabits the hazy area which is the intersection of poetry and fiction, pushing the envelope, we might say, of what can be considered a prose poem. The three pieces included here are all taken from *Anarchism Is Not Enough*, originally published in 1928 and not reprinted until 2001. ("In a Café" first appeared in *transition* a year earlier.)

Edouard Roditi (1910–1992)

In his *Thrice Chosen*, published by Black Sparrow in 1981, Roditi writes of himself:

Edouard Roditi was born in Paris in 1910 of American

parents. Educated at first in France and England, he abandoned in 1929 his studies of the Latin and Greek classics at Oxford and, until 1937, was associated with the Surrealist movement in Paris, as contributor to *transition* and to French periodicals, and as partner in Editions du Sagittaire, which published André Breton's *Surrealist Manifestos* and a number of books by Crevel, Desnos and Tzara. In 1937, he came to live in America and graduated the next year in Romance Languages from the University of Chicago, after which he pursued graduate studies there and at the University of California in Berkeley. . . . Since 1954, he has made his permanent home in Paris, but continues to travel frequently and to return regularly to the United States. (Roditi 1981, n.p.)

For this reader, Roditi is important historically because, like Paul Bowles, he serves as a link between the literary world of the twenties and that of the sixties and later. More than Bowles, however, his work in the prose poem is of inter-generational significance. The pieces published here were all taken from *New Hieroglyphic Tales* (1968) and were written, according to Roditi's foreword, starting in 1928, though most "had never been published until now." Some few had been published earlier, as he says, in "*transition, Blues,* and *Oxford Poetry 1929,*" but many others he found, years later, "in New York, in a trunk I had left there twenty years [before], together with a gray derby hat and other improbable objects that had all survived the hazards of my wandering life" (Roditi 1968, 4–5). We should be grateful, indeed, that these poems surfaced again after being lost in the storm.

Robert Alden Sanborn (1877–1966)

There is a surprising lack of information available about Robert Alden Sanborn. He was born in Boston, educated at Harvard (Class of 1900), lived for a while in New York and California, and died in Brookline, Massachusetts. In the *Harvard College Alumni Directory* for 1913, Sanborn lists his occupation as journalist. In 1917, he writes in the Contributors' Notes in the November issue of the *Poetry Journal* (Boston) that he "is at present greatly interested in the artistic possibilities of the 'Movies,' and is superintending the production in Los Angeles of some of his own photoplays."

In the Harvard College Class of 1900 *Secretary's Fifth Report* (1921), Sanborn reports the publication in 1916 of his first book, *Horizons*, by the Four Seas Company of Boston. He also lists a forthcoming title, *The Children and Judas*, due to be published in "May or June," though in fact this book remained unpublished until 1954. In a prefatory note to that volume, Sanborn refers to himself self-mockingly as "the poet laureate of baseball and the prize ring." "The Billiard Players" first appeared in *The Soil* (April 1917); "At the Elite" was first published in *The Little Review* and was reprinted in *The Children and Judas;* "Alleys" first appeared in *Others* (January 1919). In writing a eulogy on Robert Coady, editor of *The Soil*, after Coady's death in 1921, Sanborn could well have been talking about himself:

[I]t was to the play-spirit, the humor and sport of the American people, rather than to the attenuated and diluted imitations of continental schools of art, that he looked for the suggestive cultural factors that await the developing hand of the artist. Directly related to the wonders of our industrial life is the obverse and lighter side supplied by our recreative field, the games and amusements created by the skilled athletes and humorists who, challenged by the grim, grooved, work-a-day background of toil, burst forth in grace of movement and fertility of inimitable invention. (Sanborn 1922, 176–77)

Gertrude Stein (1874–1946)

However we date the start of Modernism, *Tender Buttons* represents one of the opening salvos of the new age in literature. First published in 1914 by poet Donald Evans' Claire Marie Press, *Tender Buttons* elicited a wide range of response among its literary audience. On the one hand there is Max Eastman's remark that it was a "silly book . . . equivalent in every respect except sheer passion to the ravings of a lunatic" (quoted in Hahn 1967, 166). And from William Marion Reedy, the publisher of *Reedy's Mirror*, came the following tongue-in-cheek comment: "*Tender Buttons* was so deliriously unintelligible that one printer resigned rather than continue to 'set up' her manuscript, and another was said to have committed suicide as a result of sticking to the job" (*Reedy's Mirror* 28, 42: 709).

On the other hand, there is, for example, Bob Brown's encomium, which presents a picture of the literary world before Stein blew it wide open:

At the time *Tender Buttons* was published I had to read it because positively there was nothing else in America to read. No *transition* back in 1914, no Joyce, no Cummings, no Kay Boyle, just a peep of Sandburg, no tricky little magazines of word experiment. . . . Gertrude Stein gave me a big kick. . . . That's the way you feel when you're tired to death finishing up the final paragraph of a three hundred page thriller and some blond angel slips in on a pink cloud with a cooling case of champagne. Sprays your scorched writing tonsils with it. Stein's book sprayed mine. It was a case of champagne to me in a time of dire need. (Brown 1931, 161)

Ten years later, during the twenties—when so much had happened since 1914 that you'd think *Tender Buttons* would be somewhat old hat—Kenneth Rexroth still responded to it strongly: "The explosively liberating effect of *Tender Buttons* on an adolescent modernist at the beginning of the Twenties is quite impossible to convey" (Rexroth 1966, 145). And in 1928, *transition* reprinted *Tender Buttons* in its entirety, calling it an "epochal" work. As Stein was quoted there as saying, *Tender Buttons* "was my first conscious struggle with the problem of correlating sight, sound and sense, and eliminating rhythm" (*transition* 14, Fall 1928, p. 13).

Much has been made of *Tender Buttons* in the intervening century. Intriguingly, it has been suggested that, on a coded level, it is both a record of and a reaction to the tension, sexual and emotional, that existed in the household of Gertrude, her brother Leonard, and her partner Alice B. Toklas (Kent 2003, Chapter 4).

When I asked my colleague Nickole Brown to sum up her reaction to *Tender Buttons*, she wrote:

> Sound was seated at the head of the table with meaning, work was trumped with play, repetition and pattern valued over the ordered sequence created from the long, patriarchal history of literature. For the reader to participate, she must surrender her preconceptions and expectations of what a book should do. (Personal communication, 14 October 2009)

All the selections included here are from "Objects," the first section of the book.

Jean Toomer (1894–1967)

After the Civil War, white American mainstream culture became tired of hearing about the realities of Southern black life, which had once been so prevalent in abolitionist literature. Part of the new attitude in the twentieth century was a renewal of attention to things which had been overlooked in the prosperous haze of late-nineteenth-century America, a haze which alternated with the storms of economic depression. One of the earliest literary writers to document Southern black culture, Jean Toomer collected his poems and sketches together as *Cane* in 1923. Toomer was enormously influential in the Harlem Renaissance, though he became uncomfortable with such attention.

These short pieces, Toomer said, "only come to me at intervals. Usually, after I have sketched or written a longer piece" (Toomer

2006, 83). "Calling Jesus," under the title "Nora," first appeared in the *Double Dealer* (September 1922), an issue which also included Thornton Wilder's "Sentences." "Karintha" was first published in *Broom* (January, 1923), and also shows up in Toomer's unproduced play, *Natalie Mann*—which was, according to Darwin Turner, completed in 1922 (Turner 1982, 310–12). It appears in the play as a piece read by Nathan Merilh, the semi-autobiographical protagonist.

Thornton Wilder (1897–1975)

Thornton Wilder is best known as the creator of *Our Town*. He grew up in Madison, Wisconsin, and graduated from West High School. His first published work, "Sentences," appeared initially in *The Double Dealer* (September 1922), in the same issue with Jean Toomer's "Calling Jesus." As Wilder said later, "I remember well my pride in having been accepted by *The Double Dealer*," and, as he went on to tell Frances Bowen Durrett, "you are very right in feeling that those 'little magazines' carried on the main stream of American writing" (Durrett 1964, 220). Though Durrett did include it, in its entirety, within her essay, otherwise it remained unnoticed until I rediscovered it during my doctoral research. Oddly, these two sentences reappear, in slightly different form, in Wilder's first novel, *The Cabala* (1926), where they seem no different from any other sentence in the novel (Sentence 1, pp. 31–32; Sentence 2, pp. 155–157). As they are lifted from different parts of the book, it's a mystery why or how Wilder chose those two sentences in particular to submit to a magazine—and this was, in fact, his first appearance in print. Or perhaps these two sentences served as a prompt, so to speak, upon which he later based his novel.

William Carlos Williams (1883–1963)

William Carlos Williams experimented with short prose throughout his long career. *Spring and All* (1923), for example, is a work of alternating prose and verse. In his autobiography, Williams speaks about having been intrigued, at the University of Pennsylvania (where he was a good friend of H. D. and Ezra Pound), by a work of early French literature, *Aucassin et Nicolette*, which is itself a combination of alternating verse and prose (Williams 1967, 158; Lang 1899). Williams' epic poem *Paterson* incorporates prose into it, including a letter from the young Allen Ginsberg to Dr. Williams, the famous physician-poet.

The first of his prose poems which I've included here, "The Delicacies," appeared in the *Egoist* (October *1917*), and was later included, the sole prose poem, in *Sour Grapes* (1921). *Kora in Hell: Improvisations* was published in 1920, for which, according to his autobiography, Williams paid the Four Seas Company of Boston $250 but "never received a penny, so far as I can remember, on sales" (Williams 1967, 158). The essay-like piece, "A Matisse," appeared in *Contact* 2 (January 1921), the first incarnation of a magazine edited by Williams and Robert McAlmon, and was later reprinted in *A Novellette and Other Prose, 1921–1931*, which was itself reprinted as *Imaginations* (1970). Over the years, Williams wrote several more stream-of-consciousness pieces, which he continued to call "improvisations." The one I've included here, "Theessentialroar," appeared in *transition* 10 (January 1928), and was reprinted in *Transition Workshop*, edited by Eugene Jolas (1949).

In 1932, Williams published a sequence of sixteen shorts in *Contact 1* (N.S., October 1932); this piece had the title, "For Bill Bird," who was the publisher of Three Mountains Press in Paris (the press that published the first incarnation in chapbook form of Hemingway's *in our time*). I have excerpted the first of these sketches here. This sequence was later published in a somewhat different form as "World's End," in *Life Along the Passaic River* (1938), a short story collection. As printed there, the sequentially numbered headings are replaced by a simple space between sections. Though at first they seem interrelated, the individual pieces have in fact very little to do with each other in a narrative sense, and the reader is thus forced to look for correspondences among the various fragments. "Verbal Transcription—6 A.M." and "The Pace That Kills," both of which are examples of a more traditionally narrative short, are taken from *Make Light of It: Collected Stories* (1950). The last piece included here by Williams, "Exultation," appeared in 1953 in Charles Henri Ford's "Little Anthology of the Poem in Prose," and has until now (so far as I know) never been collected.

SOURCES

Alexander, Robert. 1982. The American prose poem, 1890–1980. Ph.D. diss., Univ. of Wisconsin–Milwaukee.

Alexander, Robert, and Dennis Maloney. 2008. *The House of Your Dream: An International Collection of Prose Poetry*. Buffalo, NY: White Pine Press.

Alexander, Robert, Mark Vinz, and C. W. Truesdale. 1996. *The Party Train: A Collection of North American Prose Poetry*. Minneapolis: New Rivers Press.

Almond, Steve. 2009. "Stop." In *The Rose Metal Field Guide to Writing Flash Fiction,* edited by Tara L. Masih. Brookline, MA: Rose Metal Press.

Anderson, Margaret C. 1930. *My Thirty Years War*. New York: Covici Friede.

———, ed. 1953. *The Little Review Anthology*. New York: Hermitage House.

Anderson, Sherwood. 1918. *Mid–American Chants*. New York: John Lane. Reprint 2006, n.p.: Quale Press.

———. 1925. *Dark Laughter*. New York: Boni and Liveright.

———. 1942. *Sherwood Anderson's Memoirs*. New York: Harcourt.

———. 1989. *Sherwood Anderson: Early Writings*. Edited by Ray Lewis White. Kent, OH: Kent State Univ. Press.

Baudelaire, Charles. (1869) 1962. "À Arsène Houssaye." Dedicatory letter in *Petits poèmes en prose (Le spleen de Paris)*. Edited by Henri Lemaitre. Paris: Editions Garnier Frères.

Benedikt, Michael, ed. 1976. Introduction to *The Prose Poem: An International Anthology*. New York: Laurel–Dell.

Bergé, Carol. 1981. *Fierce Metronome: The One–Page Novels and Other Short Fiction*. NY: Window Editions.

Bernard, Suzanne. 1959. *Le Poème en prose de Baudelaire jusqu'à nos jours*. Paris: Librairie Nizet.

Beye, Holly. 1953 *In the City of Sorrowing Clouds*. San Francisco: The Greenwood Press.

———. 1955a. *XVI Poems: A Sampler*. San Francisco: The Print Workshop.

———. 1955b. *Stairwells & Marriages*. San Francisco: The Print Workshop.

———. 2006. *120 Charles Street, The Village: Journals and Writings, 1949–1950*. Huron, OH: Bottom Dog Press.

Bowles, Paul. 1972. *The Thicket of Spring, Poems 1926–1969*. Los Angeles: Black Sparrow.

Boyle, Kay. 1930. "In Memoriam Harry Crosby." *Transition 19–20* (June 1930).

———, comp. 1967. Preface to *The Autobiography of Emanuel Carnevali*. New York: Horizon.

———. 1968. *Collected Poems*. New York: Knopf.

Boyle, Kay, Laurence Vail, and Nina Conarain, eds. 1936. *365 Days*. New York: Harcourt.

Brown, Robert Carlton. 1931. *Readies for Bob Brown's Machine*. Cagnes-sur-Mer, France: roving eye press.

Burgess, Gelett. 1954. *Bayside Bohemia: Fin de Siècle San Francisco and Its Little Magazines*. San Francisco: Book Club of California.

Butler, Robert Olen. 2009. "A short short theory." *Rose Metal Press Field Guide to Flash Fiction*. Brookline, MA: Rose Metal Press, 102–103.

Caws, Mary Ann, and Hermine B. Riffaterre, eds. 1983. *The prose poem in France: Theory and practice*. New York: Columbia Univ. Press.

Chaytor, H. J. 1966. *From Script to Print: An Introduction to Medieval Vernacular Literature*. London: Sidgwick & Jackson.

Clayton, Vista. 1936. *The Prose Poem in French Literature of the Eighteenth Century*. Publications of the Institute of French Studies. New York: Columbia University.

Clements, Brian, and James Dunham. 2009. *An Introduction to the Prose Poem*. Danbury, CT: Firewheel Editions.

Cohen, Milton. 2003. "Who commissioned *The Little Review*'s 'in our time'?" *The Hemingway Review* 23.1 (Fall 2003): 106–110.

Crosby, Harry. 1931. *Sleeping together: A book of dreams*. In *American Caravan 4*, edited by Alfred Kreymborg, Lewis Mumford, and Paul Rosenfeld, 107–125. Originally published 1929[?], Paris: Black Sun Press.

Culler, Jonathan. 1978. *Structuralist Poetics*. Ithaca: Cornell Univ. Press.

Cummings, E. E. 1962. *Complete Poems, 1913–1962*. New York: Harcourt.

Dell, Floyd. 1933. *Homecoming: An Autobiography*. New York: Farrar.

Delville, Michel. 1998. *The American Prose Poem: Poetic Form and the Boundaries of Genre*. Gainesville: Univ Press of Florida.

Doolittle, Hilda [H. D.]. 1986. *Collected Poems, 1912–1944*. Edited by Louis L. Martz. New York: New Directions.

———. 1987/8. "Prose Corybantic and Four Prose Choruses." *Agenda* 25, nos. 3–4. H. D. special issue, 9–23.

Duncan, Robert. 1958. *Letters: Poems 1953–1956*. Vol. 4 of *Jargon*. Highlands, NC: Jonathan Williams.

———. 1964. *Writing, writing . . . Stein imitations?*. [Albuquerque]: Sumbooks.

———. 1968. *Derivations: Selected Poems, 1950–56*. London: Fulcrum Press.

Durrett, Frances Bowen. 1964. "The New Orleans *Double Dealer*." In *Reality and Myth: Essays in American Literature in Memory of Richmond Croon Beatty*, edited by William E. Walker and Robert L. Welker. Nashville: Vanderbilt Univ Press, 212–236.

Edson, Russell. 1980. "Portrait of the Writer as a Fat Man: Some Subjective Ideas or Notions on the Care & Feeding of Prose Poems." In *A FIELD Guide to Contemporary Poetry and Poetics*, edited by Stuart Friebart and David Young. New York: Longman, 293–302.

Eliot, T. S. 1921 "Prose and Verse." *The Chapbook—A Monthly Miscellany* 22 (April): 3–10.

———. 1957. "The Frontiers of Criticism." *On Poetry and Poets.* London: Faber, 103–118.

———. 1962. *Complete Poems and Plays.* New York: Harcourt.

———. 1996. *Inventions of the March Hare: Poems 1909–1917.* Ed. Christopher Ricks. New York: Harcourt.

Fabilli, Mary. 1968. *Aurora Bligh & Early Poems.* Berkeley: Oyez.

Faulkner, William. 1958. *New Orleans Sketches.* New Brunswick, NJ: Rutgers Univ. Press.

Finnegan, Ruth. 1977. *Oral Poetry: Its Nature, Significance and Social Context.* Cambridge: Cambridge Univ. Press.

Fitch, Noel Riley, ed. 1990. *In Transition: A Paris Anthology—Writing and art from Transition magazine 1927–1930.* New York: Doubleday.

Flanner, Janet. 1975. "A Foreword: Three Amateur Publishers." In *Published in Paris: American and British Writers, Printers, and Publishers in Paris, 1920–1939,* edited by Hugh Ford. New York: Macmillan.

Fletcher, John Gould. 1915. "Miss Lowell's Discovery: Polyphonic Prose." *Poetry* 6, no. 1 (April 1915): 32–36.

———. 1925. *Parables.* London: Kegan Paul.

———. 1930. "Education, Past and Present." In *I'll Take My Stand, by twelve southerners.* New York: Harper, 92–121.

Ford, Charles Henri, ed. 1953. "A Little Anthology of the Poem in Prose." *New Directions* 14: 329–408.

———. 1972. *Flag of Ecstasy: Selected Poems.* Los Angeles: Black Sparrow.

Fredman, Stephen. 1990. *Poet's Prose: The Crisis in American Verse.* 2nd Edition. Cambridge: Cambridge Univ. Press.

Friebert, Stuart, and David Young, eds. 1995. *Models of the Universe: An Anthology of the Prose Poem.* Oberlin, OH: Oberlin College Press.

Frost, Elisabeth Ann. 2003. *The Feminist Avant-Garde in American Poetry.*

Iowa City: Univ. of Iowa Press.

Glicksberg, Charles I. 1933. *Walt Whitman and the Civil War: A Collection of Original Articles and Manuscripts.* Philadelphia: Univ. of Pennsylvania Press.

Goldman, Emma. 1934. *Living My Life.* New York: Knopf.

Hahn, Emily. 1967. *Romantic Rebels: An Informal History of Bohemianism in America.* Boston: Houghton Mifflin.

Hall, Donald. 1977. "On Russell Edson's Genius." *The American Poetry Review* 6, no. 5 (Sept.–Oct.): 12–13.

Hansen, Harry. 1923. *Midwest Portraits.* New York: Harcourt.

Hearn, Lafcadio. (1881) 1919. "Spring Phantoms." *Fantastics and Other Fancies.* Edited by Charles Woodward Hutson. Boston: Houghton Mifflin, 147–51.

Hemingway, Ernest. 1925. *In Our Time.* New York: Boni and Liveright.

Hoffman, Frederick J., Charles Allen, and Carolyn F. Ulrich. 1946. *The Little Magazine: A History and Bibliography.* Princeton: Princeton Univ. Press.

Hunt, Leigh. 2003. *Selected Writings.* Edited by David Jesson-Dibley. NY: Routledge.

Iglesias, Holly. 2004. *Boxing inside the Box: Women's Prose Poetry.* Williamsburg, MA: Quale Press.

Jackson, Laura (Riding). 2007. *The Failure of Poetry, The Promise of Language.* Ann Arbor: Univ. of Michigan Press.

Jolas, Eugene, ed. 1949. *Transition Workshop.* New York: Vanguard.

Jolas, Eugene, and Robert Sage, eds. 1929. *Transition Stories.* New York: McKee.

Kent, Kathryn R. 2003. *Making Girls Into Women: American Women's Writing and the Rise of Lesbian Identity.* Durham, NC: Duke Univ. Press.

Knight, Brenda. 1996. *Women of the Beat Generation.* Berkeley: Conari Press.

Kreymborg, Alfred, ed. 1920. *Others for 1919: An Anthology of the New Verse.* New York: Nicholas L. Brown.

———, ed. 1930. *Lyric America: An Anthology of American Poetry,*

1630–1930. New York: Coward-McCann.

Lang, Andrew, trans. 1899. *Aucassin et Nicolette: being a love story translated out of the ancient French*. East Aurora, NY: The Roycrofters.

Lehman, David, ed. 2003. *Great American Prose Poems: From Poe to the Present*. New York: Simon and Schuster.

Lowell, Amy. 1914. "Vers Libre and Metrical Prose." *Poetry* 3, No. 6 (March 1914): 213–20.

———. 1917. *Men, Women and Ghosts*. New York: Macmillan.

———. 1918. *Can Grande's Castle*. Boston: Houghton Mifflin.

Malinowski, Bronislaw. (1922) 1978. *Argonauts of the Western Pacific*. London: Routledge.

Marek, Jayne E. 1995. *Women Editing Modernism: "Little" Magazines and Literary History*. Lexington: University Press of Kentucky.

Martinez, Elsie Whitaker. 1969. "San Francisco Bay Area Writers and Artists: An Interview Conducted by Franklin D. Walker and Willa Klug Baum." Berkeley: University of California, Regional Oral History Office, Bancroft Library.

Masih, Tara L., ed. 2009. "In Pursuit of the Short Short Story: An Introduction." *The Rose Metal Field Guide to Writing Flash Fiction*. Brookline, MA: Rose Metal Press.

Mayr, Ernst. 1969. *Principles of Systematic Zoology*. New York: McGraw-Hill.

McAlmon, Robert. 1921. *Explorations*. London: The Egoist Press.

———. 1968. *Being Geniuses Together, 1920–1930*. Revised and with supplementary chapters by Kay Boyle. Garden City, NY: Doubleday.

———. 2007. *Nightinghouls of Paris*. Champaign: Univ. of Illinois Press.

McDowell, Gary L., and F. Daniel Rzicznek, eds. 2010. *The Rose Metal Press Field Guide to Prose Poetry*. Brookline, MA: Rose Metal Press.

Merrill, Stuart, ed. 1890. *Pastels in Prose*. New York: Harper.

Meyers, Jeffrey. 1985. *Hemingway: A Biography*. New York: Harper.

Monroe, Jonathan. 1987. *A Poverty of Objects: The Prose Poem and the Politics of Genre*. Ithaca, NY: Cornell Univ. Press.

Monte, Steven. 2000. *Invisible Fences: Prose Poetry as a Genre in French and American Literature.* Lincoln: Univ. of Nebraska Press.

Moreau, Pierre. 1959. "La tradition Française du poème en prose avant Baudelaire." *Archives des lettre modernes* 3, no. 19/20 (Jan.–Feb.).

Murphy, Margueritte S. 1992. *A Tradition of Subversion: The Prose Poem in English from Wilde to Ashbery.* Amherst: Univ. of Massachusetts Press.

Patchen, Kenneth. 1957. *When We Were Here Together: Collected Poems.* New York: New Directions.

———. 1958. *Poemscapes.* Published as *Jargon 11.* Highlands, NC: Jonathan Williams.

———. 1970. *Aflame and Afun of Walking Faces.* Originally published 1953 as *Jargon 6: Fables and Other Little Tales.* New York: New Directions.

Patton, Venetria K., and Maureen Honey, eds. 2001. *Double-Take: A Revisionist Harlem Renaissance Anthology.* Piscataway, NJ: Rutgers University Press.

Poe, Edgar Allan. (1856) 1914 "The Philosophy of Composition." *The Works of Edgar Allan Poe.* Edited by E. C. Stedman and G. E. Woodberry. 10 vols. New York: Scribner's, 6: 31–46.

Rexroth, Kenneth. 1959. "Kenneth Patchen, Naturalist of the Public Nightmare." *Bird in the Bush.* New York: New Directions, 94–105.

———. 1966. *An Autobiographical Novel.* Garden City, NY: Doubleday, 1966.

Ricoeur, Paul. 1978. "Creativity in Language: Word, Polysemy, Metaphor." *The Philosophy of Paul Ricoeur.* Edited by Charles E. Reagan and David Stewart Boston: Beacon Press, 120–33.

Riding, Laura [Laura (Riding) Jackson]. [1928] 2001. *Anarchism Is Not Enough.* Edited by Lisa Samuels. Berkeley: Univ. of California Press.

Riffaterre, Michael. 1978. *Semiotics of Poetry.* Bloomington: Indiana Univ. Press.

Roditi, Edouard. 1968. *New Hieroglyphic Tales: Prose Poems.* San

Francisco: Kayak Books.

———. 1981 *Thrice Chosen.* Santa Barbara: Black Sparrow, 1981.

Rood, Karen Lane, ed. 1980. *American Writers in Paris, 1920–1939.* Vol. 4 of *Dictionary of Literary Biography.* Detroit: Gale Research.

Rosenblatt, Louise M. 1994. *The Reader, The Text, The Poem: The Transactional Theory of the Literary Work.* Carbondale: Southern Illinois Univ. Press.

Rutsala, Vern. 1978 "On Paragraphs." *Paragraphs.* Middletown, CT: Wesleyan Univ. Press, 15–18.

Sanborn, Robert Alden. 1922. "A Champion in the Wilderness." *Broom* 3, no. 3 (October 1922): 174–79.

———. 1954. *The Children and Judas, and other poems.* Boston: Bruce Humphries.

Sandburg, Carl. 1922. *Rootabaga Stories.* New York: Harcourt.

Santilli, Nikki. 2002. *Such Rare Citings: The Prose Poem in English Literature.* Madison, NJ: Fairleigh Dickinson Univ. Press.

Schneider, Isidor. 1934. "Toward Revolutionary Poetry." *Comrade: Mister.* New York: Equinox Cooperative Press, n.p.

Schwartz, Howard, ed. 1976. *Imperial Messages: One Hundred Modern Parables.* New York: Avon.

Shapiro, Karl. 197 "American Poet?" *The Poetry Wreck: Selected Essays, 1950–1970.* New York: Random House, 323–52.

Silliman, Ron 2007. *Silliman's Blog: A Weblog Focused on Contemporary Poetry and Poetics* (March 5). http://ronsilliman.blogspot.com/2007/03/ive–always–found–critical–writing–to–be.html.

Spackman, W. M. 1975. "Au fil du moi." *Parnassus* 4, No. 1 (Fall–Winter): 189–94.

Stein, Gertrude. 1914. *Tender Buttons.* New York: Claire Marie.

———. 1935. "Poetry and Grammar." *Lectures in America.* NewYork: Random House, 209–242.

Tetlow, Wendolyn E. 1992. *Hemingway's* In Our Time: *Lyrical Dimensions* Lewisburg, PA: Bucknell Univ. Press.

Thompson, Roger, ed. 1977. *Samuel Pepys' Penny Merriments.* New York: Columbia Univ. Press.

Tietjens, Eunice. 1938. *The World at My Shoulder.* New York: Macmillan.

Toomer, Jean. [1923] 1975. *Cane.* New York: Modern Library.

————. 1982. *The Wayward and the Seeking: A Collection of Writings by Jean Toomer.* Ed. Darwin T. Turner. Washington: Howard Univ. Press.

————. 2006. *The Letters of Jean Toomer, 1919–1924.* Edited by Mark Whalan. Knoxville: Univ. of Tennessee Press.

Tyler, Parker. 1953. Preface to "A Little Anthology of the Poem in Prose," edited by Charles Henri Ford *New Directions* 14.

Volkman, Karen. [2003?] "Mutable Boundaries: On Prose Poetry." http://www.poets.org/viewmedia.php/prmMID/5910.

Wagner, Linda Welsheimer. 1970. *The Prose of William Carlos Williams.* Middletown, CT: Wesleyan Univ. Press.

Williams, William Carlos. (1920) 1957. *Kora in Hell: Improvisations.* Second Edition. San Francisco: City Lights. Originally published Boston: Four Seas Co.

————. 1921. *Sour Grapes.* Boston: Four Seas Co.

————. 1923. *Spring and All.* Paris: Contact Editions.

————. 1950. *Make Light of It: Collected Stories.* New York: Random House.

————. 1967. *The Autobiography.* New York: New Directions.

————. 1970. *Imaginations.* New York: New Directions.

Young, David. 1977. *Work Lights.* Cleveland: Cleveland State Univ. Press.

ACKNOWLEDGMENTS

As this project has been thirty-some years in the making, there are a lot of people to thank. First, my gratitude goes to two men who are no longer able to read these lines: Jim Hazard, my mentor in graduate school, who many years ago encouraged my forays into the history and theory of the prose poem, and to Jim Sappenfield, former Director of Graduate Studies in the English Department at the University of Wisconsin-Milwaukee, who supported my research when others doubted its value My thanks go also to Margueritte Murphy, who found the time to honor me with an introduction to this volume. Since much of the reading that uncovered these poems occurred in the reading room of the rare book department of the Memorial Library at the University of Wisconsin-Madison, I also need to thank the staff members who willingly and cheerfully brought armload after armload of little magazines and small-press publications from the vault, and back again when I had finished with them.

Since those days, I've discussed the material I found with innumerable people, most of them no doubt having no particular interest in the prose poem, but who nonetheless listened politely. Some, like Bill Truesdale, founder of New Rivers Press, actually had an interest in the form, but I'm sure I managed to bore him anyway. More recently, Dennis Maloney, guiding spirit of White Pine Press, has indulged my obsession by agreeing to publish this volume (and by giving a home to the Marie Alexander Poetry Series), for which I am eternally grateful. My thanks also go to Nickole Brown, my co-editor at the Marie Alexander Series (which, need I say it, focuses on prose poetry), who has gone out of her way to handle the nuts and bolts of the project, despite the fact she was in the midst of moving lock, stock, and barrel to Little Rock, Arkansas, during the hottest summer on record. And last, I thank my wife, Katie Mead, who has been indefatigably ready and able to listen to all my maunderings about the prose poem for more years than I can count.

My thanks go out to all you, and to all of those I haven't mentioned who've supported me along the way. Without y'all, I could never have brought this project to fruition. But though most of the good things in this book can be laid at others' feet, the faults, as Prospero says of Caliban, are mine alone.

ABOUT THE EDITOR

Robert Alexander grew up in Massachusetts. He attended the University of Wisconsin, and for several years taught in the Madison public schools. After receiving his Ph.D. in English from the University of Wisconsin–Milwaukee, he worked for many years as a freelance editor. From 1993–1998, he was a contributing editor at New Rivers Press, and from 1999–2001 he served as New Rivers' creative director. He is currently co-editor, with Nickole Brown, of the Marie Alexander Poetry Series at White Pine Press. He divides his time between southern Wisconsin and the Upper Peninsula of Michigan.

ABOUT MARGUERITTE S. MURPHY

Margueritte S. Murphy is Acting Chair of the Writing and Rhetoric Program at Hobart and William Smith Colleges in Geneva, New York. She is author of *A Tradition of Subversion: The Prose Poem in English from Wilde to Ashbery* (The University of Massachusetts Press, 1992) and *Material Figures: Political Economy, Commercial Culture, and the Aesthetic Sensibility of Charles Baudelaire* (Rodopi, 2012), and co-editor with Samir Dayal of *Global Babel: Questions of Discourse and Communication in a Time of Globalization* (Cambridge Scholars Publishing, 2007). She has published numerous essays in journals and edited collections on nineteenth- and twentieth-century literature, and literature and economics.

COPYRIGHT ACKNOWLEDGEMENTS

THE MARIE ALEXANDER POETRY SERIES

Founded in 1996 by Robert Alexander, the Marie Alexander Poetry Series is dedicated to promoting the appreciation, enjoyment, and understanding of American prose poetry. Currently an imprint of White Pine Press, the series publishes one to two books annually. These are typically single-author collections of short prose pieces, sometimes interwoven with lineated sections, and an occasional anthology demonstrating the historical or international context within which American poetry exists. It is our mission to publish the very best contemporary prose poetry and to carry the rich tradition of this hybrid form on into the 21st century.

Series Editor: Robert Alexander
Editor: Nickole Brown

Volume 15
All of Us
Elisabeth Frost

Volume 14
Angles of Approach
Holly Iglesias

Volume 13
Pretty
Kim Chinquee

Volume 5
Moments without Names: New & Selected Prose Poems
Morton Marcus

Volume 4
Whatever Shines
Kathleen McGookey

Volume 3
Northern Latitudes
Lawrence Millman

Volume 2
Your Sun, Manny
Marie Harris

Volume 1
Traffic
Jack Anderson